Pocket
IBIZA

TOP EXPERIENCES · LOCAL LIFE · MADE EASY

Iain Stewart

In This Book

QuickStart Guide

Your keys to understanding Ibiza – we help you decide what to do and how to do it

Need to Know
Tips for a smooth trip

Regions
What's where

Explore Ibiza

The best things to see and do, region by region

Top Experiences
Make the most of your visit

Local Life
The insider's Ibiza

The Best of Ibiza

Ibiza's highlights in handy lists to help you plan

Best Walks
See Ibiza on foot

Ibiza's Best...
The best experiences

Survival Guide

Tips and tricks for a seamless, hassle-free Ibiza experience

Getting Around
Travel like a local

Essential Information
Including where to stay

Our selection of Ibiza's best places to eat, drink and experience:

◎ **Experiences**

✖ **Eating**

⬡ **Drinking**

✪ **Entertainment**

⬡ **Shopping**

These symbols give you the vital information for each listing:

♪ Telephone Numbers		✦ Family-Friendly
⊙ Opening Hours		❀ Pet-Friendly
P Parking		▢ Bus
◎ Nonsmoking		⊠ Ferry
@ Internet Access		M Metro
⬙ Wi-Fi Access		S Subway
⬩ Vegetarian Selection		▢ Tram
▢ English-Language Menu		▢ Train

Find each listing quickly on maps for each region:

Bar Hemingway

16 ⬡ Map p233, B2

Legend has it that Hemi self, wielding a machine ...rate this timber-pan ...ered bar during ... showpiece is a ...en by Papa ar ... town. Dress ...s.com; Hôtel Rit ... ⊙6.30pm-2a

6 ◎ Plac Vς

Lonely Planet's Ibiza

Lonely Planet Pocket Guides are designed to get you straight to the heart of the destination.

Inside you'll find all the must-see sights, plus tips to make your visit to each one really memorable. We've split the destination into easy-to-navigate regions and provided clear maps so you'll find your way around with ease. Our expert authors have searched out the best of the destination: walks, food, nightlife and shopping, to name a few. Because you want to explore, our 'Local Life' pages will take you to some of the most exciting areas to experience the real Ibiza.

And of course you'll find all the practical tips you need for a smooth trip: itineraries for short visits, how to get around, and how much to tip the guy who serves you a drink at the end of a long day's exploration.

It's your guarantee of a really great experience.

Our Promise

You can trust our travel information because Lonely Planet authors visit the places we write about, each and every edition. We never accept freebies for positive coverage, so you can rely on us to tell it like it is.

QuickStart Guide 7

Explore Ibiza 21

Worth a Trip:

The Best of Ibiza 127

Ibiza's Best Walks

Ibiza's Best...

Survival Guide 145

QuickStart Guide

Welcome to Ibiza

World renowned for its clubbing scene, Ibiza offers much more than DJ-driven dance floors and teenage kicks. A hippy heritage still resonates in the less-developed north of the island (and in neighbouring Formentera), while Ibiza Town is culturally sophisticated and outrageously picturesque. Factor in remote cove beaches, family resorts and a cosmopolitan dining scene, and its appeal is unique.

Ibiza
Top Experiences

Dalt Vila (p24)

A focal point for the whole island, the spectacular walled enclave of Dalt Vila occupies the high ground in Ibiza Town and contains a roster of cultural sight

Port Area (p28)

Formerly a fishers' quarter, the whitewashed houses and narrow lanes of Ibiza Town's Port Area are today replete with stylish bars and hip boutiques, and include a gay village.

Botafoc & Talamanca (p32)

On the north side of Ibiza Town is the natural habitat of the island's high rollers, with a millionaires' marina, the fine beach of Talamanca and restaurants galore.

Puig de Missa (p52)

A fortified hilltop above the town of Santa Eulària des Riu, Puig de Missa contains a beautiful 13th-century church, an ethnographic museum and offers sweeping vistas of the east coast.

Salines Beach & Salt Flats (p102)

The shimmering salt pans of Ses Salines are a haven for bird life. Wonderful Salines beach, inside a natural park, has a breathtaking stretch of sand and some of the island's very best *chiringuitos* (beach bars).

Sant Antoni's Coastal Surrounds (p84)

Several delectable bays fringe the town of Sant Antoni, including Calas Conta and Comte. Heading west, Cala Bassa is a lovely cove with inviting turquoise water.

SEBASTIA TORRENS / GETTY IMAGES ©

JUERGEN SACK / GETTY IMAGES ©

Northern Beaches (p64)

Ibiza has over 30 idyllic cove beaches, and it's a near-impossible task to name the best. Explore the options and find your best beach.

Es Vedrà & Around (p98)

Rising like a mini-volcano from the Mediterranean, this island is the source of many legends, including a claim to be Homer's island of the sirens.

r-Hopping in San An (p86)

nt Antoni is the most popular resort
Ibiza, drawing tens of thousands of
ng party-minded British punters
ry year. There are still plenty of
re mellow places to enjoy a relaxed
nk, on the Sunset Strip and dotted
und town, too.

Trucador Peninsula (p116)

Blessed with sugar-white sands and
lapped by turquoise seas, Formentera's remarkable back-to-back
beaches of Illetes and Llevant are a
vision of paradise.

ant Carles de Peralta (p62)

Ibiza's northeast, this tranquil
ttlement has a quintessentially
izan church, and an interesting bar
two.

Sant Rafel (p46)

Best known for the two megaclubs
Amnesia and Privilege, Sant Rafel
also has some good restaurants
and cafes.

Ibiza
Local Life

Insider tips to help you find the real regio

After checking off Ibiza and Formentera's top sights, here's how you can experience what makes the islands tick – the hip local hang-outs, charming villages, sunset bar and quirky local shops that comprise a unique lifestyle.

Nightcrawlers' Ibiza Town (p34)

▶ Funky bars
▶ Club parades

Sassy, cosmopolitan Ibiza Town has a glut of drinking dens. With tranquil bars on Plaça des Parc, superb harbourfront terraces in the Port Area and Ibiza's very own gay village, you won't go thirsty. Troops of costumed club-sponsored parades add fantasy to the Ibizan night.

Hanging Out in Santa Gertrudis (p66)

▶ Smart restaurants
▶ Church

This easy-going village has a roll-call of restaurants and cafes that's out of proportion to its size (but in keeping with its wealthy catchment area). Check out the quirky auction house for antiques and curios, and allow plenty of time for people-watching.

Off-the-Beaten-Track Coves (p68)

▶ Secret beaches
▶ Dramatic scenery

Northern Ibiza is less developed than the south and boasts some spectacular coves. This route takes in several special bays, all of them isolated, and two of which – Cala d'Aubarca and Portitxol – involve a short hike to reach.

Road-Tripping Southern Coves & Villages (p104)

▶ Diverse landscapes
▶ Landmark sculpture

This extraordinary drive across Ibiza's south begi by the horizon-filling sa flats, skirts an archaeological site, a towering forested peak and two hidden cove beaches, before a grand finale at a site locals have christene 'Stonehenge'.

Gay Pride Parade on Ibiza

Bar Costa (p67), Santa Gertrudis

Other great places to experience the islands like a local:

Ibiza
Day Planner

Day One

Begin the day with an Ibizan breakfast of coffee and a *tostada* at **Madagascar** (p39) in Ibiza Town, then tour Dalt Vila's sights including the superb **Museu d'Art Contemporani** (p25), the highly informative **Madina Yabisa La Cúria** (p25), and the Gothic **Catedral** (p26) that enjoys a fine view over the city.

Head south to stunning **Platja de ses Salines** (p103) for a swim and some people-watching, then catch some Balearic tunes and lunch at **Sa Trinxa** (p130). Be sure to pause and admire the nearby Salines salt pans. Then it's a trip west to take in a sunset over the island **Es Vedrà** (p99) from the isolated **Torre des Savinar** (p99) watchtower.

In the evening, head up to **La Paloma** (p77) in Sant Llorenç for exquisite mod-Med cuisine, then back to Ibiza Town for drinks in the port and, for those with the stamina, the dance floor at **Pacha** (p43).

Day Two

Head for the Botafoc marina and grab a table at **Organic Market** (p41) for breakfast with a view, followed by a beautiful drive up the island's eastern coast via Cala Llonga before exploring the sights of Santa Eulària's **Puig de Missa** (p52).

Continue north to the exquisite little cove of **Cala d'en Serra** (p65), where you can lunch at the shoreside *chiringuito* (beach bar) and enjoy a lazy afternoon on the beach. Pack a mask and snorkel, as the water is fabulously clear here. Returning south, consider a drink in **Anita's bar** (p80) in the delightful village of Sant Carles, also home to boutiques and a handsome village church.

You can't beat the relaxed evening vibe around the village square in prosperous Santa Gertrudis, home to numerous cafes, bars and restaurants. Take your pick: the Italian food at **Macao** (p67) is superb or, for more of a healthy eating menu, **Wild Beets** (p67) is excellent, too.

hort on time?

Ve've arranged Ibiza's must-sees into these day-by-day itineraries to make sure you
ee the very best of the island in the time you have available.

Day Three

Today it's a fantastic day trip to Formentera. On arrival, sort yourelf out with a scooter or bicycle then addle up and head for the pretty village **Sant Francesc Xavier** (p124). Browse s boutiques, including **Muy** (p123), nen grab a juice and light bite at **Ca Na epa** (p121). Next it's up to the **Trucador eninsula** (p116) to relish its blinding hite-sand beaches and turquoise seas. rom here you can wade over to **Espalador** (p117) and check out the island's nud pool and defence tower.

In the late afternoon bike it to the far east of the island, the pennsula of La Mola, famous for its lonely **ghthouse** (p119). Be sure to enjoy the istas from **Codice Luna** (p121) here. hen head over to Platja de Migjorn for sundowner at **Blue Bar** (p123), before atching an evening boat back to Ibiza.

From the ferry port in Ibiza it's a short walk to **Locals Only** (p40) or dinner. Then explore the nearby bouques and bars of the **Port Area** (p28).

Day Four

Take an excursion to the north and west of the island. Start with breakfast in **Giri Café** (p74) in the atmospheric village of Sant Joan, then head up to **Portinatx** (p73) for a midmorning stroll along a lovely shoreside trail to its isolated **lighthouse** (p74), from where Mallorca is visible on clear days.

Then it's a trip along the coast to the lovely cove of **Benirràs** (p65), a sheltered inlet surrounded by wooded hills. Dine on seafood here, then snooze (or swim) your lunch off. If it's a Sunday, hang around till sunset and you'll witness a drumming ceremony attended by many of Ibiza's bohemian crowd.

In the early evening enjoy a civilised drink in the wonderful rural hotel **Atzaró** (p142), followed by a hearty meal at **Camí de Balàfia** (p74), which specialises in grilled meats. Alternatively, head to Sant Antoni's **Sunset Strip** (p94) for a sundowner, followed by dinner at **El Chiringuito** (p92).

Need to Know

For more information, see Survival Guide (p145)

Currency
Euros (€)

Language
Catalan and Spanish

Visas
Not needed for EU citizens. Citizens of Australia, Canada, Israel, Japan, New Zealand and USA do not require a visa for visits of up to 90 days.

Money
ATMs widely available. Credit cards accepted in most hotels, restaurants and shops.

Mobile Phones
Local SIM cards can be used in European and Australian phones. Visitors from other countries (including the USA) may need tri-band or quadric-band phones.

Time
Central European Time (GMT/UTC plus one hour)

Plugs & Adaptors
Plugs have two round pins; electrical current is 220V.

Tipping
Not expected in bars or cafes but small change is appreciated. In restaurants 10% is sufficient for good service.

① Before You Go

Your Daily Budget

Budget less than €100

▶ Room in a hostel €40–€60

▶ *Bocadillo/tostada* and catering from supermarkets €10

▶ Travelling by bus to beaches and villages €1.50–€4

Midrange €100–€200

▶ Comfortable double room from €70

▶ Rental car from €20 per day

▶ Evening meal with wine €25–€35

Top End more than €200

▶ Stylish boutique or *agroturisme* hotel from €140

▶ Admission to club €30–€70

▶ Gourmet dining with wine from €40

Useful Websites

▶ **Ibiza Spotlight** (www.ibizaspotlight.com) Highly informative, with active forums.

▶ **Ibiza Voice** (www.ibiza-voice.com) Strong on the club scene.

▶ **Essential Ibiza** (www.essentialibiza.com) Reviews and discounted club tickets.

▶ **Lonely Planet** (www.lonelyplanet.com/spain/ibiza) Destination information, hotel bookings and traveller forum.

Advance Planning

Six months before Book flights early for the best price; reserve accommodation for high season.

Two weeks before Book tables for top restaurants.

One week before Organise discounted club tickets in advance.

② Arriving in Ibiza

om Ibiza's airport you can either take a taxi
 bus, or arrange a rental car, to get to your
stination. In high season prepare yourself
 a long wait to catch a taxi (which are in
ort supply) or to get your car rental agree-
ent organised.

↘ From Ibiza Airport

estination	Best Transport
iza Town and erry Terminal or Formentera	Bus L10
ant Antoni	Bus L9
anta Eulària	Bus L24
ant Josep	Bus L9

om La Savina Port, Formentera

ings are very mellow at the little port of La
vina, where all boats to Formentera arrive.
u'll be faced with rows of rental companies
 offering bicycles and scooters for rent;
ese are the best way to explore the island.
ses stop directly outside, too.

③ Getting Around

The best way to get around Ibiza is undoubtedly by car, which will give you the flexibility
to pick and choose where and when you
want to go. Similarly, Formentera is far more
accessible if you've got your own wheels
(whether a car, scooter or bicycle). Both
islands do have a reasonable bus services,
which connect all the main towns, though on
many routes buses are infrequent.

🚗 Car Hire

For the best rates book a car in advance
online. There are many local agencies based
in and around the airport.

🚲 Bicycle & Scooter

Formentera is (mostly) very flat and perfect
to explore by pedal power or on a scooter.
Ibiza is far more hilly.

🚕 Taxi

Taxis are an excellent way to get around
(except between mid-July and late August
when demand outstrips supply). Check www.
ibizaairport.org for sample fares. Expect to
pay around €16 from the airport to Ibiza
Town; fares increase at night.

🚌 Bus

Ibiza and Formentera's bus network is pretty
efficient, particularly if you base yourself in
one of the main towns. But if you're staying
in the countryside or want to visit remote
beaches, services are very irregular or non-
existent; consult www.ibizabus.com. Clubbers can use the excellent **Discobus** (www.
discobusibiza.com) service in high season.

⛴ Ferry

Ibiza and Formentera are connected by
regular ferries (every 30 minutes between
May and October). Ibiza also has little ferry
boats which connect the main towns with
nearby beaches.

Ibiza
Regions

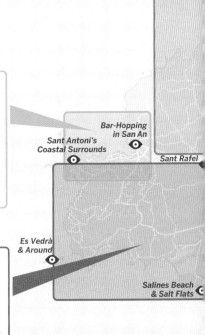

Sant Antoni de Portmany & Around (p82)
The main town in the west is a party-geared resort; it's close to some outstanding beaches.

◉ Top Experiences

Sant Antoni's Coastal Surrounds

Bar-Hopping in San An

Southern Ibiza (p96)
Utterly compelling to explore, the south has spectacular sights and several superclubs.

◉ Top Experiences

Es Vedrà & Around

Salines Beach & Salt Flats

Formentera (p114)
The last word in tranquillity and barefoot living, this small island is a paradise for naturists and naturalists.

◉ Top Experiences

Trucador Peninsula

Bar-Hopping in San An ◉

Sant Antoni's Coastal Surrounds ◉

Sant Rafel

Es Vedrà & Around ◉

Salines Beach & Salt Flats ◉

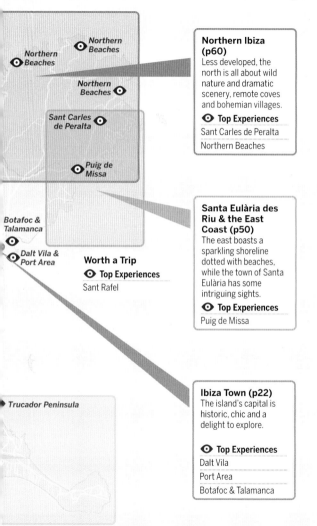

Northern Beaches

Northern Beaches

Northern Beaches

Northern Beaches

Sant Carles de Peralta

Puig de Missa

Northern Ibiza (p60)
Less developed, the north is all about wild nature and dramatic scenery, remote coves and bohemian villages.

Top Experiences
Sant Carles de Peralta
Northern Beaches

Botafoc & Talamanca

Dalt Vila & Port Area

Worth a Trip
Top Experiences
Sant Rafel

Santa Eulària des Riu & the East Coast (p50)
The east boasts a sparkling shoreline dotted with beaches, while the town of Santa Eulària has some intriguing sights.

Top Experiences
Puig de Missa

Trucador Peninsula

Ibiza Town (p22)
The island's capital is historic, chic and a delight to explore.

Top Experiences
Dalt Vila
Port Area
Botafoc & Talamanca

Explore
Ibiza

View up to Dalt Vila's Catedral (p26), Ibiza Town
WESTEND61 / GETTY IMAGES ©

Explore

Ibiza Town

The heart and soul of the island, this Unesco-listed World Heritage site is spectacular to look at, a shopaholic's dream and a hedonist's paradise. Ibiza Town's boutiques and bars attract a unique blend of characters, and in the summer months it becomes one of the world's greatest catwalks, as fashionistas and clubbers strut around its warren of whitewashed lanes.

The Region in a Day

☀ Start the day in a cafe on **Plaça des Parc** (p38) or Vara de Rey with the quintessential Ibiza breakfast: a coffee and a *tostada* (toasted baguette, smeared with ripe tomato). Visit **Casa Broner** (p29) and then head up into historic **Dalt Vila** (p24), pausing to visit its museums, **ramparts** (p25), **Catedral** (p26) and viewpoints.

☀ In the afternoon stroll over to the Botafoc marina for a dose of yacht envy before lunching by the shore at either **Organic Market** (p41) or nearby **Bar Flotante** (p40). Then find a patch of sand on Talamanca beach and loaf away the rest of the afternoon.

☾ Ibiza Town at night is something to behold. First browse the Port Area, dipping in and out of boutiques. Dine at **S'Escalinata** (p39) or **Locals Only** (p40), then stroll along the spectacular harbourfront, pausing to admire the club parades from a table at **The Rock** (p35). Take a walk on the wild side on Carrer de la Verge, home to Ibiza's gay village and myriad funky shops. Finally it's off to **Pacha** (p43) to get your groove on.

For a local's day in Ibiza Town at night, see p34.

 Top Experiences

◯ **Local Life**

♥ **Best of Ibiza Town**

Getting There

🚌 **Bus** L10 from airport (every 15–20 min Jun–Oct, every 30 min Nov–Apr).

🚌 **Bus** L3 from Sant Antoni (every 15–30 min Jun–Oct, every 30–60 min Nov–Apr).

🚌 **Bus** L13 from Santa Eulària (every 20 min Jun–Oct, every 30–60 min Nov–Apr).

There are reduced services on Sundays; consult www.ibizabus.com.

Top Experiences
Dalt Vila

Its floodlit bastions visible from across southern Ibiza, Dalt Vila is a fortified hilltop that was first settled by the Phoenicians and later occupied by a roster of subsequent civilisations. Tranquil and atmospheric, many of its lanes are only accessible on foot. It's mostly a residential area, but it also contains several key cultural sights. The best way to explore is to enter via the Portal de ses Taules gateway and wind your way uphill: all lanes lead to the cathedral-topped summit.

◉ Map p36, D4

admission free

🚌 45

Portal de ses Taules (p26)

Don't Miss

Ramparts

Encircling Dalt Vila, Ibiza's **colossal protective walls** reach over 25m in height and include seven bastions. Evocatively floodlit at night, these fortifications were constructed to safeguard Ibiza's residents against the threat of pirate attack. You can walk the entire perimeter of this impressive Renaissance-era ramparts, designed to withstand heavy artillery. Along the way, enjoy great views over the Port Area and south to Formentera.

Museu d'Art Contemporani (MACE)

Housed within an 18th-century powder store and armoury, **Museu d'Art Contemporani** (Map p36, E3; www.mace.eivissa.es; Ronda de Narcís Puget; admission free; ⏾ 10am-2pm & 5-8pm Tue-Fri, 10am-2pm Sat & Sun Apr-Jun & Sep, 10am-2pm & 6-9pm Tue-Fri, 10am-2pm Sat & Sun Jul & Aug, 10am-4.30pm Tue-Fri, 10am-2pm Sat-Sun Oct-Mar) is a showcase for contemporary art, most of it with an island connection. The permanent collection contains work by Ibizan artists Marí Ribas Portmany and Tur Costa, and the abstract art of Ibiza visitors Will Faber and Erwin Broner. There are also Japanese prints and photographs. Descend to the archaeological site to map out Ibiza's history through the ages – from the Phoenicians to the Islamic period.

Madina Yabisa La Cúria

This **small display** (Map p36, E4; Carrer Major 2; adult/child €2/free; ⏾ 10am-2pm & 6-9pm Tue-Fri, 10am-2pm Sat & Sun) replicates the medieval Arab city of Madina Yabisa (Ibiza Town), prior to the island's fall to Catalan forces in 1235. Artefacts, audiovisuals and maps transport visitors back in time. The centre is housed in what was, from the 15th century, the Casa de la Cúria (law courts). Parts of its

---

☑ Top Tips

▸ You can walk Dalt Vila's entire ramparts in less than an hour.

▸ Aside from the grand gateway Portal de ses Taules there are three other entrances to this walled enclave, including the impressive Portal Nou.

▸ Dalt Vila makes a spectacular location for dinner; you'll find several restaurants in Plaça de Vila and Sa Carrossa.

▸ You can't drive into Dalt Vila; only residents' vehicles (and buses) are allowed access. Take bus L45 from Vara de Rey.

✗ Take a Break

The pretty cafe-bar S'Escalinata (p39) has low tables and cushioned seating on a steep stone staircase. Or fortify yourself for the climb up to Dalt Vila at Croissant Show (p40).

interior have been exposed to reveal the original Arab-era defensive walls.

Portal de ses Taules

A stone ramp leads from the Mercat Vell up to the **Portal de ses Taules** (Map p36, E4), the main entrance to Dalt Vila. Above it hangs a plaque bearing Felipe II's coat-of-arms and an inscription recording the 1585 completion date of the fortification. The gateway is flanked by two statues, replicas from Ibiza's Roman era, which add to its grandeur.

Catedral

Ibiza's **Catedral** (Map p36, E5; Plaça de la Catedral; admission free; ⊘9.30am-1.30pm & 4-8pm), which sits near the highest ground in Dalt Vila, elegantly combines several styles: the original 14th-century structure is Catalan Gothic, the sacristy was added in 1592, and a major baroque renovation took place in the 18th century. Inside, the **Museu Diocesà** (Plaça de la Catedral; admission €1.50; ⊘9.30am-1.30pm Tue-Sun, closed Dec-Feb) contains some impressive religious art.

Catedral

Understand

Ibiza's Walls & Castle

Ibiza's Defensive Walls

Ibiza Town's towering, foreboding defensive walls were constructed in the 16th century in a desperate bid to safeguard the citizens from Turkish and Moorish pirate attack. Ringing the entire historic quarter of Dalt Vila, they were completed in 1585 and remain in excellent condition.

The Carthaginians first built walls on Dalt Vila's high ground around the 5th century BC, fortifications that were later extended during the Moorish era – you can get an excellent perspective of the town at this time in the Madina Yabisa La Cúria exhibition (and view sections of the original Moorish walls). Other walls from this period can be seen below the Baluard de Sant Jordi.

In the 16th century, after centuries of damage at the hands of pirates, Ibiza's crumbling defences were completely rebuilt and extended. Huge new fortifications were designed by Giovanni Battista Calvi and Jacobo Fratín, including seven colossal bastions (baluards).

Today the walls of Dalt Vila – at almost 2km long, 25m high and up to 5m thick – are some of Europe's best-preserved fortifications, and form a key part of the city's Unesco World Heritage recognition.

The Historic Castle

Occupying the very highest ground in Dalt Vila, Ibiza's semiderelict castle is actually an assortment of historic buildings (built over a 1000-year period), including the Arab-era Tower of Homage, a former governor's residence, the 8th-century Almudaina (a Moorish keep) and, on the western side, infantry barracks that date from the 18th century.

The best view of the structure is from the huge bastion Baluard de Sant Bernat, on the southern side of Dalt Vila's ramparts. Today the castle's facade has been restored (after decades of neglect) and its interior largely stabilised, though long-term plans to convert the building into a luxury parador hotel have stalled.

During the Spanish Civil War, mainland Anarchists massacred over a hundred Ibizan Nationalist prisoners here before fleeing the island.

Top Experiences
Port Area

The Port Area of Ibiza Town has an immediate and addictive appeal. Wandering this highly atmospheric warren of tottering old fishers' houses and cobbled streets, replete with achingly hip fashion boutiques and quirky market stalls, is an essential Ibiza experience.

The quarter is not loaded with conventional sights; the fun is simply soaking up the summer scene from a harbourside terrace, and watching the party people and outrageous club parades. For here, the night is pure theatre, as the routine is derided and the excessive celebrated.

👁 Map p36, G3

Getting There

🚌 **Bus** There's no service into the heart of the Port Area, but buses L10, L12A and L15 stop on Avinguda Santa Eulària, just to the west.

Sa Penya district, Port Area

Don't Miss

Carrer de la Verge

Running parallel to the harbourfront, this tiny 400m-long lane is named for the Virgin Mary, though these days it's dedicated to bacchanalian pleasures more than religious devotion. **Carrer de la Verge** (Sa Penya) forms Ibiza's main gay village, with around 20 or so bars (many are cavelike spaces, seemingly hacked out of the hillside).

There's also a smattering of gay-orientated boutiques and a restaurant or two. During July and August the tiny streetside terraces are packed with drinkers and there's a heady ambience as the sultry Ibiza night is celebrated long into the wee hours.

Passeig Marítim

This elegant harbour **promenade**, remodelled in 2015, showcases Ibiza Town's magnificent waterfront, and is lined with cafes, bars and restaurants. It's a delight to explore; yachts bob about on the marina on the north bank, while whitewashed old fisher's homes fill its south side. At the eastern end of the prom a breakwater extends into the harbour.

Casa Broner

Formerly the private home and studio of architect Erwin Broner (1898–1971), this modernist Sa Penya apartment is now open to the public. Broner, who was Jewish, fled from Nazi Germany to Ibiza in 1934 and designed numerous houses around the island. Several of Broner's drawings are exhibited inside. Elegant and understated, **Casa Broner** (Map p36, H3; Sa Penya 15; 10am-2pm Tue-Sun, 5-8pm Tue-Fri Apr-Jun & Sep, ⊘10am-2pm Tue-Sun, 6-8pm Tue-Fri Jul & Aug, 10am-4.30pm Mon-Sat, 10am-2pm Sun Oct-Mar) enjoys fine sea and port views from

☑ **Top Tips**

▶ This zone is very quiet during the winter months, between November and Easter.

▶ Harbourfront bars tend to charge much more for drinks than those just inland; bars on Plaça des Parc are moderately priced.

▶ The dark lanes above (south of) Carrer de la Verge comprise a poor *barrio* (district) where street crime can occasionally be an issue. Be careful after dark.

✗ Take a Break

Madagascar (p39) is the ideal place to refuel with a coffee or juice (or something stronger). There's no traffic to contend with near its lovely terrace.

its roof terraces and whitewashed living area.

Mercat Vell

Fruit and vegetables have been traded at the neoclassical **Mercat Vell** (Map p36, E3; Plaça de sa Constitució; ⏱9am-9.30pm May-Oct, to 6pm Nov-Apr), or 'Old Market', since 1873. Today most of the produce, which includes olive oil and artisan breads, is locally sourced. Cafes and bars fringe the market.

Corsair Monument

Midway along Passeig Marítim, this **stone obelisk** (Map p36, F2) is a monument to Ibiza's corsairs, privateers licensed by the Spanish crown to combat the threat of pirates. It faces a small square, Plaça d'Antoni Riquer, named after a legendary Ibizan corsair.

Corsair Monument

Understand

Moorish Ibiza

The Moors made irregular raids on Ibiza and the Balearics in the 8th and 9th centuries AD (and collected some taxes), but they did not take formal control until 902, when the Emir of Córdoba launched an invasion of the islands. At the time of the Moorish conquest Ibiza was a poor, isolated backwater, with minimal links to the outside world. Arab rule brought many benefits, above all specialised irrigation systems, which transformed the agricultural sector, enabling crops such as rice and sugar cane to be grown, and enabling the production of two harvests a year in the fields of Ses Feixes.

Ibiza Town thrived during Moorish rule, becoming a prosperous port with bustling markets. The town gained a new name (Yabisa), a new language (Arabic) and a new religion (Islam). Yabisa was divided into three zones during the Moorish period, with the castle and palace boasting their own fortifications at the top, a middle residential and market zone, and a lower area that bordered the port. Most of Ibiza Town's defensive walls that border the port were established during the Moorish period. The excellent audiovisual displays inside Madina Yabisa La Cúria are highly informative about this era.

For 200 years the town, under tolerant *walis* (governors), was generally prosperous and stable. Away from Yabisa, ancient ways survived in the island's rural areas, and Christianity was practised clandestinely. Trouble erupted when control of the Balearics passed to the Almortadha dynasty of Arab governors in 1085. The Almortadha raided towns in mainland Spain and Italy from bases in the Balearics, provoking a massive invasion of Ibiza in 1114. Thousands of troops from hundreds of Pisan and Catalan ships, backed by the pope, formed a minicrusade. Though Christian forces massacred most of the island's Muslim population and ended Almortadha rule, they didn't take control of the islands, and two subsequent (more benign) Moorish ruling dynasties, the Almoravids and Almohads, regained power.

Moorish rule came to an end when Catalan forces took the citadel of Yabisa on 8 August 1235 after a long siege. Catalan replaced Arabic as the main language, Catholicism became the official religion, and Yabisa was renamed Eivissa.

Top Experiences
Botafoc & Talamanca

The upmarket Botafoc area on the north side of Ibiza's harbour contains a roster of luxury apartment blocks, a casino, a yacht club and marina, and the clubs Lío (p44) and Pacha (p43). There's a sprinkling of cafes and restaurants, many with fine harbour and Dalt Vila views, too. Just north of Botafoc is Talamanca beach, a half-moon bay with golden sands, safe swimming in shallow waters, a hotel or two, and some good places to eat.

Getting There
🚌 **Bus** L12B from Ibiza Town (every 60 min).

⛴ **Boat** Shuttle (May–Oct) from Passeig Marítim, Ibiza Town.

Luxury hotel, Talamanca

Don't Miss

Talamanca Beach
This sandy bay is the best beach within walking distance of Ibiza Town. Tourism development has not been too unkind to Talamanca, with hotels mainly located on its northern and southern fringes. There's good swimming, with very sheltered waters. A clutch of shoreside restaurants adds to Talamanca's allure.

Botafoc Marina
Forming the northern part of Ibiza Town's harbour, the Botafoc marina is one of Europe's most exclusive, full of gleaming yachts. Jutting into the bay between the boats is Lío (p44), a club-cabaret venue, while cafe-restaurants fringe the harbour waters.

Ses Feixes
On the western side of Talamanca beach, the scruffy-looking fields of reeds and scrub known as **Ses Feixes** (admission free) were once Ibiza Town's vegetable garden. These were developed by the Moors over a thousand years ago, and irrigated using innovative water management techniques and crop rotation, which enabled two crops a year.

Botafoc Peninsula
Beyond the marina is the narrow Botafoc peninsula, home to Ibiza's main ferry terminal. A lighthouse marks the easternmost point; this is the focus for celebrations when hundreds gather here to see the first sunrise of the new year.

Nearby: s'Estanyol
Something of a secret beach, s'Estanyol is a delightful, if tiny, cove, only accessible by a rough road. By the shore there's a *chiringuito* (beach bar; May to October) for meals, drinks and occasional after parties. Offshore you'll find excellent snorkelling. From the north side of Talamanca beach follow the signpost; the last 2km is a dirt track.

☑ Top Tips

▶ Talamanca beach is sheltered and very shallow, so it's ideal for kids who aren't strong swimmers.

▶ On weekends during the summer months Talamanca gets very busy with families from Ibiza Town. You may want to try more isolated beaches which are less packed.

▶ Talamanca beach is just a couple of kilometres south of the village of Jesús, home to a handsome church which dates back to 1466.

✗ Take a Break

With affordable prices and a setting right by the shore, Bar Flotante (p40) is an excellent venue for fish and seafood, a *bocadillo* (filled roll), or just a beer or glass of rosé with a view. Or revive your spirits with Organic Market's (p41) marina views and healthy menu.

Local Life
Nightcrawlers' Ibiza Town

The port is by far Ibiza's most rewarding and atmospheric area for
an evening out. Kick off in intimate
Plaça des Parc, before heading
east along the harbourfront to
enjoy a drink on one of the terraces there. Then head back along
gay-friendly Carrer de la Verge and
finish up on Carrer d'Alfons XII,
where the club parades terminate.

❶ Hostal Parque
At the western end of Plaça des
Parc, **Hostal Parque** (☎971 30 13 58;
hostalparque.com; Plaça des Parc 4; ☺8am-
midnight; 🛜) is a smart cafe-bar. It's
the perfect place to plan a night on
the town, with good-quality *cava* (€16
bottle) and well-prepared mojitos
and caipirinhas (€8.50), plus snacks
(including good salads). All kinds of
characters, from yachtie types to hardcore clubbers, frequent the terrace.

❷ Teatro Pereira

Just east of the Plaça des Parc the **Teatro Pereira** (www.teatropereyra.com; Carrer del Comte de Rosselló 3; ◷8am-4am; 📶) is a time warp: all stained wood and iron girders. It was once the foyer of a long-abandoned 1893 theatre – the ruined remains are at its rear. The Pereira is often packed and offers nightly live music.

❸ Can Pou

Can Pou (📞971 318 826; Carrer Lluís Tur i Palau 19; ◷noon-4pm & 8pm-midnight; 📶) is one of the port's most dependable harbourfront bars, attracting a loyal local crowd thanks to its moderate prices and the fact that it's open all year. The interior is atmospheric (it's in a historic building), but it's the great marina-facing terrace that's Can Pou's real appeal. Live music some nights, and tapas are served, too.

❹ The Rock

This is the meeting point in the port zone for club promoters and dance-music-industry types, so it's a good bet for finding out what's on and bumping into a DJ or two (and perhaps even scoring a free club entrance pass – ask the friendly bar staff). **The Rock** (Carrer Garijo 14; ◷8pm-3am May-Oct) has a superb harbourfront terrace, and all the club parades pass here at some stage in the night.

❺ Sunrise

One of the most popular gay bars on the 'Street of the Virgin', **Sunrise** (📞677 489827; Carrer de la Verge 44; ◷8pm-4am daily Apr-Nov, 8pm-4am Sat Dec-Mar) has a gorgeous interior (and even more gorgeous bar staff). Try out the swings by the bar (don't fall off!). Friendly and welcoming, with a decadent cocktail list and live DJs some nights. Sunrise also draws a hip hetero and lesbian crowd.

❻ Bar 1805

Tucked away on a Sa Penya backstreet, this terrific boho bar has the best cocktails in town. There's lots of absinthe action on the list – try a Green Beast (served in a punch bowl) or the house margarita (with mescal instead of tequila), which packs a mean Mexican punch. **Bar 1805** (📞651 625972; www.bar1805ibiza.com; Carrer de Santa Llucía 7; ◷8pm-3.30am May-Oct; 📶) also has a great outdoor terrace.

❼ Soap at Dome

A legendary gay bar, famous as the final destination for the club parades which so define the Ibiza night. Around midnight in the summer months, the **Soap at Dome** (📞971 19 18 38; Carrer de Santa Llúcia 21; ◷10pm-3.30am Apr-Oct) terrace is pure theatre as costumes are rated and there's a joyous buzz in the night air. Expect the unexpected, as gold-paint sprayed dancers, fluffy pink bunnies, bondage queens and leather kings, bearing club banners and dispensing promo flyers, jostle for acclaim and attention.

A

B

C

D

1

C de Carles III

26 30 15 10

Botafoc
Talama

C de Pere Francès

22

C de Felipe II

C de Carles V

Av de Santa Eulària

2

Av d'Isidor Macabich

Av d'Ignasi Wallis

Av de Bartomeu Rosselló

C del Comte de Rosselló

34

19
16

C de Madrid

C de Vicent d'Austria

C de Juan Cuervo

C Ramon i Cajal

C C
Rian

C C
To

3

C del Bisbe Carrosco

C de l'Historiador
Josep Clapés

C d'Aragó

Av de Bartomeu Vicent Ramón

Vara de Rey
Monument

Pg de Vara de Rey

5

C B
Az

18
13

Av d'Espanya

Pg de Vara de Rey

9

35

Plaça
des
Parc

1

C d'Avicena

C Pere Sala

25

4

C del Canonge Joan Planells

C de la Vía Púnica

C de Cayetano
Soler

12

Baluard d'es
Portal Nou

6

C de sa Murada

C Santa Cre

C de Rosari

Dalt

C Vía Romana

C de Sant Josep

C de la Conquista

C de Joan Rom

C de Sant
Ciràc

4

Museu
Puget

2

Necròpolis
del Puig
des Molins

C del Bes

Baluard de
Sant Jaume

Pa
Episc

Almud

5

17 3

Ronda de Joan Baptista

Baluard de
Sant Jordi

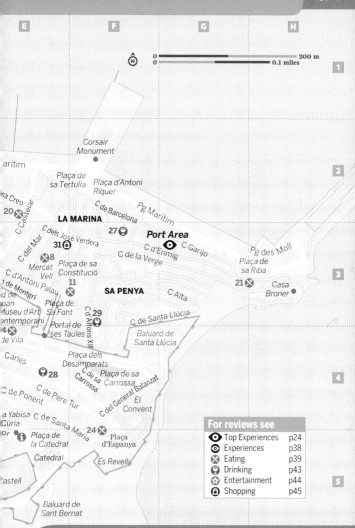

E | F | G | H

0 ——————————— 200 m
0 ——————————— 0.1 miles

Corsair
Monument

arítim

Plaça de
sa Tertulia

Plaça d'Antoni
Riquer

sa Creu
C Castelar
20

C de Barcelona

Pg Marítim

LA MARINA

C dels José Verdera

27

Port Area 🔴

C de la Verge

C d'Enmig

C Garijo

Pg des Moll

Plaça de
sa Riba

31

C del Mar

Mercat
Vell

Plaça de sa
Constitució

8

SA PENYA

C Alta

21

Casa
Broner

C d'Antoni Palau
d de Montgri
Museu d'Art
ontemporani
4
de Vila

Plaça de
Sa Font

C d'Alfons XIII

29

Portal de
ses Taules

C de Santa Llúcia

Baluard de
Santa Llúcia

Carles

Plaça dels
Desamparats

28

C de sa
Carrossa

Plaça de sa
Carrossa

C del General Balanzat

C de Ponent

C de Pere Tur

El
Convent

a Yabisa
Cúria

C de Santa Maria

24

Plaça
d'Espanya

Plaça de
la Catedral

Catedral

Es Revellí

astell

Baluard de
Sant Bernat

Experiences

Plaça des Parc

SQUARE

1 Map p36, D3

The bohemian heart of Ibiza Town, this pretty square is traffic-free and lined with cafe-bars and restaurants. Grab a table and simply take it all in as club promoters discuss DJ line-ups, coiffured ladies feed their poodles titbits, clubbers grumble about comedowns and buskers sing for their supper. (Plaça des Parc)

Necròpolis del Puig des Molins

HISTORIC SITE

2 Map p36, A4

The earliest tombs within this ancient burial ground date from the 7th century BC and Phoenician times. Follow the path around and peer into the *hypogea* (burial caverns), cut deep into the hill. You can descend into one interlocking series of these. The recently renovated site museum displays finds such as amulets and terracotta figurines discovered within the more than 3000 tombs that honeycomb the hillside.

At the time of research, this museum also housed exhibits from the **Museu Arqueològic** (Plaça de la Catedral 3; adult/child €2.40/free; ☺10am-2pm & 6-8pm Tue-Sat, 10am-2pm Sun) in Dalt Vila (which was closed for renovation). (www.maef.es; Carrer Via Romana 31; adult/child €2.40/free; ☺10am-2pm & 6.30-9pm Tue-Sat, 10am-2pm Sun)

Figueretes

BEACH

3 Map p36, B5

Southwest of Dalt Vila, the slender beaches of the Figueretes neighbourhood are the nearest to the capital. There's a palm-lined promenade, several sea-facing restaurants and, of course, the opportunity for a dip in the sea.

Museu Puget

MUSEUM

4 Map p36, D4

A historic mansion with a typical late-Gothic courtyard and staircase that houses 130 paintings by Ibizan rtist Narcís Puget Viñas (1874–1960) nd his son, Narcís Puget Riquer 1916–83). (Carrer Major 18; admission free; ⊙10am-2pm & 5-8pm Tue-Sun Apr-Jun & Sep, 10am-2pm & 6-8pm Tue-Sun Jul & Aug, Oam-4.30pm Tue-Fri, 10am-2pm Sat-Sun Oct-Mar)

Vara de Rey Monument STATUE

 5 Map p36, D3

This statue depicts the Ibizan General Joachim Vara de Rey, who died in the 1889 Battle of Caney, fought between Spain and the USA over Cuba. It's located on the island's most beautiful boulevard, which is graced with elegant townhouses. (Vara de Rey)

Eating

S'Escalinata MEDITERRANEAN, CAFE €

6 Map p36, C4

Enjoying an incredibly scenic location inside Dalt Vila, this casual cafe-restaurant's low tables and cushioned seating (on the steps of a steep stone staircase) create a relaxed vibe. Healthy breakfasts, tapas and *bocadillos* (filled rolls) are offered. It's open late, so doubles as a bar late into the night with good house sangria and cocktails. (☎971 30 61 93; www.sescalinata. es; Carrer Portal Nou 10; snacks/meals from €5/9; ⊙10am-3.30am Apr-Oct; ☎)

Comidas Bar San Juan MEDITERRANEAN €

7 Map p36, E3

More traditional than trendy, this cramped, atmospheric family-run operation harks back to the days before Ibiza became a byword for glam and glitz. It offers outstanding value, with fish and grilled meat dishes for around €10. No reservations, so arrive early and expect to share your table with others. (Carrer de Guillem de Montgrí 8; mains €7-11; ⊙1-3.30pm & 8.30-11pm Mon-Sat)

Bistrot El Jardin CAFE €

8 Map p36, E3

Pot plants and herbs fill the terrace of this cafe on the market square. It's a laid-back spot for fresh-pressed juices and smoothies, and we love their creative take on salads – from goat's cheese with pears, nuts and honey to artichoke hearts with endives and gorgonzola, which are attractively presented on slate. (Plaça de sa Constitució 11; light meals €7-15; ⊙8am-1am, closed Sun in winter)

Madagascar CAFE, BAR €

9 Map p36, C3

Probably the most popular bar-cafe on traffic-free Plaça des Parc, this enjoyable place is great for a juice (try an orange and carrot mix), baguette (from €3.50) or a tapa or two. In the evening it's more of a relaxed bar, with inexpensive *combinados* (spirit with mixer) and draught beer. (📞971 55 55 55; Plaça des Parc; snacks €2-8; ⏰9am-2am May-Sep, to 11.45pm Oct-Apr; 📶)

Bar Flotante
SPANISH €

10 Map p36, D1

Offering tables so close to the sea that you can almost dip your toes in the Mediterranean as you eat your meal, this restaurant is always popular. Prices are moderate, with fresh fish and grilled meats, snacks and good house wines. (📞971 19 04 66; Platja Talamanca; snacks €3-8, meals from €8; ⏰9am-11.30pm)

Croissant Show
CAFE €

11 Map p36, F3

Opposite the food market, this is where *everyone* goes for an impressive range of pastries, gourmet salads and post-partying breakfast goodies. It is quite a scene all on its own. Grab a table on the people-watching terrace. (📞971 31 76 65; Plaça de sa Constitució; snacks/light mains from €2/9; ⏰6am-11pm; 📶)

Locals Only
MEDITERRANEAN €€

12 Map p36, D3

Situated on pretty Plaça des Parc, this restaurant gets rave reviews from locals for its Mediterranean food and moderate prices. There's a pretty terrace (perfect for people-watching), an attractive interior, and staff are professional and informed. Daily specials

are chalked up on a board (such as yellowtail tuna carpaccio) or try any of the pasta dishes. House wines are well selected and priced. (📞971 30 19 97; Plaça des Parc 5; mains €12-19; ⏰noon-1am)

El Parador
PARRILLA €€

13 Map p36, A3

Located next to a busy road on the suburban outskirts of Ibiza Town (3km west of the centre), this unassuming Argentinian-owned place is a carnivor's delight with grilled meats perfectly cooked over charcoal on a custom-built *parrilla* (grill). Try the *entraña* (€16) or a full *parrillada* (€22); portions are huge and come with a side salad and thin-cut fries. (📞971 30 05 36; Carrer Portinatx 2; meals €12-22; ⏰8pm-midnight Tue-Sun)

El Olivo

MEDITERRANEAN €€

14 Map p36, E4

Standing head and shoulders above most places inside the walled city, this slick little bistro has plenty of pavement seating in wonderfully atmospheric Plaça de Vila. The modern Mediterranean menu goes with the seasons in strong flavours like rack of lamb in a fennel-mustard crust or roasted cod with spicy chorizo – all delivered with finesse. Book ahead. (☎ 971 30 06 80; www.elolivoibiza.org; Plaça de Vila 7; mains €17-26, tapas menu €28; ⏰ 7pm-1am Tue-Sun)

Organic Market

HEALTH FOOD €€

15 Map p36, D1

This pretty cafe-restaurant enjoys vistas over the marina and offers a healthy menu featuring organic ingredients and vegetarian and vegan options. It's superb for a breakfast buffet (€9.50) which includes spelt-flour bread and freshly squeezed juices, or you can enjoy dishes like *pollo de corral* (roasted freerange chicken with quinoa risotto) later in the day. (☎ 971 19 27 26; Botafoc marina; meals €11-24.50; ⏰ 8am-midnight; 📶 🥢)

Can Terra

TAPAS €€

16 Map p36, B2

A stylish tapas bar, with a sandstone walled-interior and lovely rear garden, that's rammed most nights with locals devouring delectable tapas (from €3) and dishes such as *sepia a la plancha* (grilled cuttlefish; €10.50), and quaffing *cañas* (draught beer) and rosé wine. Be prepared to wait a while for a table. (☎ 971 31 00 64; Avinguda d'Ignasi Wallis 14; meals €12-18; ⏰ 8.30am-2am)

Soleado

FRENCH €€

17 Map p36, B5

Figueretes' promenade has a stack of mediocre restaurants, but happily Soleado is definitely a cut above the rest. The menu is Provençal, with fine fish (like grilled turbot with saffron sauce), seafood and meat; the set menu is €24. There's a delightful shoreside terrace so you can eat right by the sea. Figueretes is a 15-minute walk southwest of the centre. (☎ 971 39 48 11; www.soleadoibiza.com; Passeig de ses Pitiuses, Figueretes; meals €24-38; ⏰ 1-3.30pm & 7.30pm-midnight)

Bar 43 Tapas

TAPAS €€

18 Map p36, A3

This cosy, unfussy bar distinguishes itself with its warm welcome and generously portioned tapas – *gambas al ajillo* (prawns sautéed in garlic), *boquerones* (marinated anchovies) and the like. Go for the good buzz and reasonable prices. (☎ 971 30 09 92; www.ibiza-43.com; Avinguda d'Espanya 43; meals €15-18; ⏰ 8pm-2am Mon-Sat; 📶)

Mar a Vila

TAPAS €€

19 Map p36, B2

This sweet tapas place brings a dash of the sea to the city centre and conceals a pretty inner courtyard. The tapas and *pintxos* (Basque tapas) are bang on the money, as are satisfying mains like sticky pork cheeks with carrot-potato cream and macadamia nuts. Check out the set menu (€15) for excellent value for money. (Avinguda d'Ignasi Wallis 16; mains €9-15; ⏰10am-midnight Mon-Sat)

Taberna el Gallego

GALICIAN €€

20 Map p36, E2

With exposed stone walls and long wooden benches this place looks like your typical north Spanish restaurant and, as the name suggests, it specalises in tasty tapas and seafood dishes from Galicia in the wave-lashed northwest corner of Spain. (Carrer Castelar 7; mains €14, tapas €4-8; ⏰noon-4pm & 7-11.30pm)

Thai'd Up

THAI €€

21 Map p36, H3

Boasts a prime location at the eastern end of the Port Area, and there's an expansive terrace to enjoy authentic Thai curries, noodle dishes and stir-fries. Prices are moderate considering the location, with all the club parades passing by in high season. (📞971 19 16 68; Plaça de sa Riba 11; mains €12-18; ⏰7pm-2am May-Oct)

S'Ametller

IBIZAN €€€

22 Map p36, B1

The 'Almond Tree' specialises in local, market-fresh cooking. The daily menu (for dessert, choose the house *flaó*, a mint-flavoured variant on cheesecake and a Balearic Islands speciality) is inventive and superb value. S'Ametller also offers cookery courses – including one that imparts the secrets of that *flaó* (📞971 31 17 80; www.restaurantsametller.com; Carrer de Pere Francès 12; menus €24-38; ⏰1-4pm & 8pm-1am Mon-Sat, 8pm-1am Sun)

La Torreta

MEDITERRANEAN €€€

23 Map p36, E3

La Torreta offers some of the best cuisine, particularly seafood and desserts, in Dalt Vila. Eat on the large front terrace, or for a really special setting, book the dining room that occupies one of the Dalt Vila's medieval defence towers. Service is great but it does get very busy, so book ahead in high season. (📞971 30 04 11; Plaça de Vila 10; mains €16-32; ⏰6.30pm-1am daily May-Sep)

Restaurant of Hotel Mirador de Dalt Vila

MEDITERRANEAN €€€

24 Map p36, F5

At this intimate – do reserve – restaurant with its painted barrel ceiling and original canvases around the walls, you'll dine magnificently. Service is discreet yet friendly, and dishes are creative, colourful and delightfully presented. Allow time to sip

Pacha nightclub

n aperitivo in the equally cosy bar;
at your feet is an underfloor display
of antiquities recovered from the sea.
(☏971 30 30 45; Plaça d'Espanya 4; menú
€45, mains €26-30; ⏱Easter-Dec; 🛜)

La Brasa   MEDITERRANEAN €€€

25 🍴 Map p36, D3

La Brasa's forte is its quality fish and
meat, cooked to perfection, and its paella
is another speciality. There's a lovely terrace, shaded by vines, palms and banana
trees and adorned with bursts of bougainvillea. Perhaps best visited outside
the high season months (when service
and the kitchen are pressed). (☏971 30
12 02; www.labrasaibiza.com; Carrer Pere Sala 3;
mains €18-32; ⏱1-4pm & 7-11.45pm)

Drinking
Pacha   CLUB

26 🍺 Map p36, C1

Established in 1973, Pacha is Ibiza's
original, and most classy nightclub.
It's the only venue that remains open
all year and is the islanders' party
venue of choice. Built around the shell
of a farmhouse, it boasts an amazing
main dance floor, funky room, huge
VIP section and myriad other places
to groove or chill, including a fab
open-air terrace and restaurant.

Virtually anyone who's anyone
in the DJ world has manned the
decks here including the likes of Paul
Oakenfold, Sasha and Roger Sanchez.

Cherry-pick your night: David Guetta's F*** Me I'm Famous is the hottest ticket in town. There are now dozens of Pacha clubs spread around the world, from Shanghai to New York, and the brand has established a worldwide reputation for a chic, Balearic brand of clubbing. (www.pacha.com; Avinguda 8 d'Agost; admission €30-70, drinks from €12; ⏱11pm-6am daily May-Sep, 11pm-6am Sat Oct-Apr)

La Tierra
BAR

27 🚇 Map p36, F3

Just off Carrer Barcelona in the Port Area this cave-like bar was a prime hippy hang-out back in the day. The ambience remains lively with hard-drinking locals mixing with visiting clubbers. DJs spin funk, lounge and tech-house. (Passatge Trinitat 4; ⏱9pm-3am May-Oct; 📶)

Anfora
GAY

28 🚇 Map p36, E4

Seemingly dug out of walls of rock, this is the best-known gay dance haunt high up Dalt Vila, with wild party nights: from strip shows to disco nights. Draws an international, older crowd with DJs playing queer anthems, house and R 'n' B. (www.discoanfora.com; Carrer Sant Carles 7; admission €15-20; ⏱midnight-6am May-Oct)

Angelo
GAY

29 🚇 Map p36, F3

In the shadow of the old city walls, Angelo is a busy gay bar with several levels. The atmosphere is relaxed and heteros wind up here, too. Nearby are a handful of other gay-leaning bars. (www.angeloibiza.com; Carrer d'Alfons XII 11; ⏱10pm-4am May-Oct)

Entertainment

Lío
CABARET, LIVE MUSIC

30 ⭐ Map p36, D1

This venue enjoys the best location in Ibiza: from its terraces there are perfect views of Dalt Vila. It's aimed at an older crowd, featuring gourmet dining, cabaret shows and live music. After 1am it morphs into more of a club. Reserve ahead.

Expect to shell out some serious cash (upwards of €120) for a night out

Top Tip

Clubbing Outside Ibiza Town

Just 6km east of Ibiza Town, the inland village of Sant Rafel is home to two of the world's most acclaimed clubs. Amnesia (p47) is legendary, for this is where the **Balearic Beat** (a mix of acid house, indie, funk and disco) music explosion kicked off in the late 1980s. The club retains an underground, alternative reputation. Over the road is the monumentally proportioned Privilege (p47), the world's largest nightclub, which was home to wild Manumission nights for over a decade.

here. There's no entrance charge as such: a dinner reservation includes all entertainment. (www.lioibiza.com; Passeig Joan Carles I; 7pm-6am May-Sep)

Shopping

Antik Batik
CLOTHING

31 Map p36, E3

This French label specialises in gorgeous kaftans (from around €250), bold prints, sandals and items which have an ethnic look. They also sell stylish bags, jewellery, shoes and scarves. (971 31 57 06; Plaça de sa Constitució 8; 10am-11pm May-Sep)

Revolver
CLOTHING

32 Map p36, D3

Extraordinary lycra bodysuits, sunglasses with moon-inspired frames and terrific designer gear from the likes of Thom Krom, Marc Jacobs and Vivienne Westwood. Also slides and sandals, hi-top trainers and very cool hats. (971 31 89 39; www.revolveribiza.com; Carrer Bisbe Azara 2; 11am-11pm)

Divina
CLOTHING

33 Map p36, D4

This Dalt Vila boutique specialises in Ibizan Ad Lib style (loose-fitting white clothing) that's perfect for the island's summer climate. You'll find items for men, women and kids. (971 30 11 57; Carrer Santa Creu 7; 11am-2am May-Oct)

Local Life
Sombrería Bonet

Established in 1916 **Sombrería Bonet** (Map p36, D3; 971 31 06 68; Carrer del Comte de Rosselló 6; 10am-2pm & 5-8pm Mon-Sat) is a hat shop that sells an amazing selection of headgear, including panamas, trilbies, berets and cowboy hats in traditional styles (and also in contemporary colours). Most are in the €18 to €60 range. Woven bags from natural fibres are also stocked.

Pacha
CLOTHING

34 Map p36, D2

There are now Pacha stores across the island (and beyond) but you can't beat shopping a stone's throw from this global superclub's HQ. Stocks bags, accessories, mixed CDs and clothing for men, women and kids. (971 31 35 35; www.pachacollection.com; Carrer de Lluís Tur i Palau 20; 10am-11.30pm May-Sep)

Natural 2
FOOD & DRINK

35 Map p36, C3

Partying hard? This health store stocks a roster of supplements, and nutritional support: vitamins, minerals, 'immune enhancers', antioxidants, amino acids as well as gluten- and sugar-free produce. (971 30 20 75; bioeivissa.com; Plaça des Parc 1; 10am-2pm & 5-8pm Mon-Fri, 10am-2pm Sat)

Top Experiences
Sant Rafel

Getting There

🚌 **Bus** L3 (every 15 to 30 minutes May to October; every 30 to 60 minutes November to April) connects Sant Rafel with both Ibiza Town and Sant Antoni.

Close to the centre of the island, surrounded by some of the most fertile land in Ibiza, the small village of Sant Rafel is equidistant from the raunchy bar action and high-rises of Sant Antoni, and the classy nightlife and cosmopolitan culture of Ibiza Town. Its two blockbuster sights are both night-clubs. If you've no interest in dance-floor action, there's also a lovely village church, an eco-centre, and several good places to eat here.

Privilege nightclub

Don't Miss

Amnesia

Amnesia (www.amnesia.es; Carretera Ibiza a Sant Antoni Km 5; admission €35-70; ⏰midnight-6am May-Oct) is arguably Ibiza's most influential club, its decks welcoming DJ royalty such as Sven Väth, Paul Van Dyk, Paul Oakenfold and Avicii. The club's origins actually go back to the 18th century, when the farmhouse the club has been built around was first constructed. It was a venue for hippy gatherings in the 1970s, then became Ibiza's first after-hours club in the mid-1980s, with Balearic tunes played in the sunshine by the legendary DJ Alfredo. Amnesia's underground, innovative musical policy made it the most fashionable club in the island.

Today there's a warehouse-like main room and a terrace topped by a graceful atrium. Big nights include techno-fest Cocoon; Cream; foam-filled Espuma, which always draws a big local crowd; and La Troya, the biggest gay night on the island.

Privilege

The world's biggest club, **Privilege** (www.privilege ibiza.com; Sant Rafel; admission €25-60; ⏰11pm-6am May-Sep) is a mind-blowing space that regularly hosts 10,000 clubbers. The venue was originally an open-air affair called Ku: stars including Freddie Mercury and James Brown headlined. Privilege's best times were undoubtedly during Manumission's infamous residency (1994–2007), which featured ground-breaking theatrics (including live sex shows). DJs Tiesto and Armin van Buuren have also enjoyed successful seasons here.

The main dance floor is an enormous, pulsating area, where the DJ's cabin is suspended above the crowd. VIP zones are located on upper levels, while an open-air dome forms a chill-out zone.

☑ Top Tips

▶ There are ATMs in the village.

▶ If you're clubbing, don't attempt to run across the busy Ibiza–Sant Antoni highway to get a bus connection as deaths have occurred; use the bridges.

▶ You'll find several ceramic workshops and pottery shops in the village to browse.

✗ Take a Break

Spending too long inside nightclubs and need a healthy reboot? Check out the **Rabbit Hole** (☎971 19 88 20; rabbit holeibiza.com; Avinguda Isidoro Macabich, Sant Rafel; meals €8-16; ⏰11.30am-5.30pm Mon-Fri; ✗). This cafe-restaurant offers a 100% organic, gluten-free menu. Mediterranean, Asian and Middle Eastern recipes feature strongly.

Pick your night carefully; sometimes this vast venue can feel achingly empty. In the Vista room (also known as the Coco Loco zone), DJs spin alternative sounds, and in the back room there are sometimes live acts.

Dining Out

Opposite the village church, **Clodenis** ([☎]971 19 85 45; Carrer Pintor Narcís Puget, Sant Rafel; meals €28-50; [🕑]8.30pm-1am Mon-Sat Apr-May, daily Jun-Oct, Wed-Sat Nov-Mar) is an excellent Provençal restaurant with a lovely outdoor terrace and atmospheric dining rooms; the cuisine is consistently good and the wine list extensive. Or you could try **Ca'n Pilot** ([☎]971 19 82 93; www.asadorcanpilot.com; Carretera Vieja Eivissa a Sant Antoni, Sant Rafel; meals €18-32; [🕑]1-4pm & 8pm-midnight), on the village high street, for delicious Spanish-style grilled meats, with excellent lamb, *pollo payés* (country chicken) and beef. Order the *chuletón* (T-bone steak) for two and they'll bring a small grill to your table so you can cook the cuts of salted beef yourself.

Església de Sant Rafel

Sant Rafel's typically Ibizan **church** (admission free) is perched on a hilltop some 300m or so east of the village's high street. Built in the late 18th century, its brilliantly whitewashed facade and walls make it a local landmark, particularly when the structure is floodlit at night. There's a pretty little plaza by the church, from where there are fine views down to Dalt Vila and the east coast of the island.

Nearby: Casita Verde

Casita Verde ([☎]971 18 73 53; [🕑]2-7pm Sun) is an ecological education facility and permaculture centre 6km southwest of Sant Rafel. It's also the headquarters of Greenheart Ibiza, an environmental charity. Visitors are welcome (Sundays only) to tour its bottle houses, and to drink in the juice bar – try a 'health booster' with aloe vera, honey, mint and lemon. It's a tricky place to find; consult its website.

Understand

The Story Behind Ibiza's Clubs

In Ibiza, historically clubs 'leased' their premises to outside promoters on different nights. British dance brands introduced this initiative in the 1990s, at the height of the superclub era, when cash-rich clubs such as Ministry of Sound descended en masse to the White Isle. So Thursdays found Cream (from Liverpool) at Amnesia (p47; in Ibiza). We Love parties at Space (p111) on Sundays reached near-legendary status, with British promoters taking over the club for a 22-hour (8am to 6am!) marathon clubbing session. These 'leasing' arrangements still continue to a degree, but today the Ibizan clubs generally prefer to promote their own nights, working directly with DJs rather than via outsiders.

The most successful outside promoter in the island's clubbing history was undoubtedly Manumission (Latin for 'freedom from slavery'), who were resident in Sant Rafel's Privilege (p47) club for 14 years between 1994 and 2007. On Manumission nights the venue regularly pulled in 10,000 punters, and this was the night out that visiting clubbers could not miss.

Manumission (the team consisted of two brothers, Andy and Mike McKay, and their partners Dawn and Claire, plus an army of PR people) started as a gay night in Manchester, but after violent threats from gangsters they set up shop in Ibiza. Instead of paying huge fees to superstar DJs, they concentrated on creating a fantasy event at Privilege, with acrobats, circus performers, cabaret, actors and dancers (and such kookiness as a DJ in the toilets). The night climaxed with a live sex show starring Mike and Claire. Unsurprisingly, the British and Ibizan papers granted Manumission an avalanche of publicity; journalistic outrage sparked record ticket sales and resulted in a club rammed to the rafters.

After a dispute with Privilege, Manumission briefly shifted over the road to Amnesia, but tensions between the brothers led to a split. Andy and Dawn later set up the very successful Ibiza Rocks, introducing live bands to Ibiza (including Arctic Monkeys and the Libertines) and turning the legendary Pike's hotel (p92) into a key party venue. Mike and Claire returned to the clubbing arena with a night called Phantasmagoria in the 2013 and 2014 seasons, but the event suffered licensing issues. Both couples still live in Ibiza, and are raising families on the island.

Explore

Santa Eulària des Riu & the East Coast

Santa Eulària des Riu is an attractive coastal town with an easy-going vibe, a large marina, a fine promenade and a small historic quarter concentrated on the Puig de Missa hilltop. It also boasts a famous 'street of restaurants' (Carrer Sant Vicent). Close by are some lovely beaches, including Cala Llonga, Cala Llenya, Cala Boix and the tiny cove of Cala Mastella.

The Region in a Day

Begin with breakfast at **Passion** (p56) on Santa Eulària's promenade and then head up to the town's **Puig de Missa** (p52) to tour its sights: the **church** (p53) and **Museu Etnogràfic** (p53). Revel in the vistas over the east coast and its wooded hills.

Now, set off in search of the perfect beach. There are a string of jewels on the northeast coast: take your pick from Cala Pada, Cala Nova, Cala Llenya, Cala Boix and tiny Cala Mastella. Mastella's shoreside restaurant, **El Bigotes** (p57), is the perfect spot for lunch.

In the evening head over to the sheltered bay of **Cala Llonga** (p55) for a cocktail and reggae music in the **Jam Shack** (p58), before dining on the sea-facing terrace at nearby **Amante** (p58), one of the island's most beautiful restaurants.

👁 Top Experiences
Puig de Missa (p52)

🖤 Best of Santa Eulària des Riu & the East Coast

Eating
Amante (p58)

Drinking
Jam Shack (p58)

Shopping
Queens of Joy Fashion (p59)

Getting There

🚌 **Bus** L13 from Ibiza Town (every 20 min Jun–Oct, every 30–60 min Nov–Apr).

🚌 **Bus** 19 from Sant Antoni (eight daily Mon–Sat Jun–Oct, two daily Mon–Sat Nov–Apr).

Top Experiences
Puig de Missa

This hilltop was a perfect retreat for the town's citizens during the centuries when Ibiza was plagued by pirate attacks. Crowning its 52m summit is a remarkable fortress-church, complete with its very own defence tower. There are a couple of interesting museums to visit, too. You can walk up to the Puig de Missa via an interpretive trail which runs from Santa Eulària's promenade to its Ajuntament (Town Hall); the route is clearly marked with information boards.

⊙ Map p54, B3

Getting There

Walk Puig de Missa is a 10-minute walk west of the town's Plaça d'Espanya.

Don't Miss

Església de Puig de Missa

This beautiful fortified **church** (admission free; ⊙9am-9pm May-Oct) dates from 1568. Its most impressive features are its defence tower (used as a shelter during pirate attacks) and entrance porch (complete with mighty supporting pillars). Inside, its interior is simple and whitewashed throughout, except for the dramatic churrigueresque-style altar. Mass is held on Sundays at 11am.

Museu Etnogràfic

The **Museu Etnogràfic** (☎971 33 28 45; Can Ros, Puig de Missa; adult/child €3/free; ⊙10am-2pm & 5.30-8pm Tue-Sat Apr-Sep, mornings only in winter) concentrates on Ibiza's rural heritage and occupies a stunning old *casament* (farmhouse). In its *porxo* (long room) are carpentry tools and musical instruments including drums made from pine and animal skins. Other exhibits include billowing wedding dresses and ceremonial necklaces, a huge olive oil press and a privateer's licence.

Nearby: Riverside

Santa Eulària gets its suffix, 'des Riu' (of the river), from this reed-fringed stream just west of Puig de Missa. Normally there's little more than a trickle of water, but it *is* the only river in the Balearics. Check out Can Planetes (p55) for information about irrigation and the pleasant riverside trail via the Pont Vell (old bridge) to the seafront.

☑ Top Tips

▶ As there are no cafes or restaurants on Puig de Missa, bring some bottled water.

▶ Approach via Carrer Pintor Barrau and Carrer Sol and you'll pass the town's small marketplace.

▶ Avoid the heat of the day: it's best to visit in the morning when the museums are open.

▶ The steps up to Puig de Missa are steep – the elderly and those with mobility issues may struggle.

✕ Take a Break

In the centre of town Royalty (p59) is great for drinks and snacks, while on the promenade Passion (p56) has a line-up of excellent juices and healthy food.

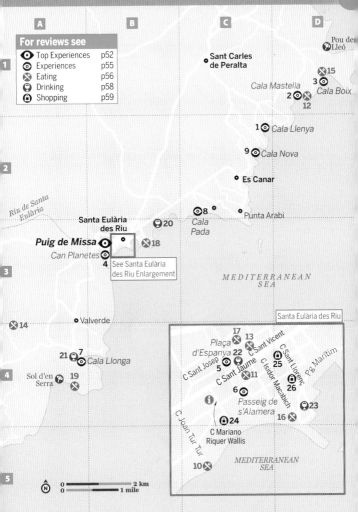

A B C D

For reviews see
- Top Experiences   p52
- Experiences   p55
- Eating   p56
- Drinking   p58
- Shopping   p59

Pou des Lleó

Sant Carles de Peralta

15 3
Cala Mastella   Cala Boix
2 12

1 Cala Llenya

9 Cala Nova

Es Canar

8   Punta Arabí
Cala Pada

Puig de Missa
Santa Eulària des Riu   **20**
18
Can Planetes   **4**
See Santa Eulària des Riu Enlargement

MEDITERRANEAN SEA

14   Valverde

21 7
Cala Llonga
Sol d'en Serra   **19**

Santa Eulària des Riu

17 13
Plaça d'Espanya **22**   C Sant Vicent
C Sant Josep **5**   C Sant Llorenç
C Sant Jaume   **25**
11   C Isidor Macabich
6   **26**
Passeig de s'Alamera   **23**
24   **16**
C Mariano Riquer Wallis
10   MEDITERRANEAN SEA

Pg Marítim

N   0   2 km
0   1 mile

Experiences

Cala Llenya
BEACH

1 Map p54, C2

Situated 9km northeast of Santa Eulària, Cala Llenya is a serene pine-fringed sandy bay (around 200m wide) popular with French, German and local families – though it never seems to get too crowded. Easterly breezes mean the water can get wavy here.

Cala Mastella
BEACH

2 Map p54, D1

This lovely little cove beach is set at the back of a deep inlet where pine trees reach down and almost kiss the bay's emerald-green water. Outside high season you could have the beach totally to yourself. Scramble around the rocks at the northeastern end to reach the acclaimed El Bigotes (p57) seafood restaurant.

Cala Boix
BEACH

3 Map p54, D1

Below a highly scenic coastal road, this slimline beach has dark coarse sand and pebbles. It's quite exposed, so if there's an easterly or north wind blowing things can get choppy. Steps lead down from the cliffs to the shore. You'll find a couple of good restaurants above the beach, including La Noria (p57).

Can Planetes
MUSEUM

4 Map p54, B3

This information centre, located in a restored mill, explains the irrigation systems which were first developed by the Moors and flourished along Santa Eulària's riverbank. It's just off the town's Passeig des Riu (riverbank promenade). (Passeig des Riu; admission free; ⊙10am-1pm Tue-Sun)

Plaça d'Espanya
PLAZA

5 Map p54, C4

This palm tree-studded square contains Santa Eulària's dignified Ajuntament (Town Hall), built in 1795; its frontal colonnade is flanked by two municipal coats-of-arms. Can Cosmi (p58), a meeting point for locals and visitors, faces the square. (Plaça d'Espanya)

Passeig de s'Alamera
AREA

6 Map p54, C4

Passeig de s'Alamera is Santa Eulària's mini-Ramblas, a graceful boulevard lined with trees and cafes. During the main tourist season market stalls add plenty of colour, selling jewellery, clothing and local produce. (Passeig de s'Alamera)

Cala Llonga
BEACH

7 Map p54, A4

Bordered by wooded headlands to the north and south, Cala Llonga is a very sheltered bay. It's primarily a family resort with a sandy beach and wonderful swimming; however, the huge concrete hotels disfigure the scene somewhat.

Cala Pada
BEACH

8 Map p54, C2

About 2km northeast of Santa Eulària, fringed by pine groves and villas, this attractive beach has fine, pale sand and shallow water ideal for safe swimming. You'll find three cafe-restaurants at the back of the bay (and sunbeds are for hire for €4.50/day). Hourly boats connect the beach with Santa Eulària in the summer.

Cala Nova
BEACH

9 Map p54, C2

Just north of the resort of Es Canar, this exposed sandy beach (around 250m long) sits pretty on a wide bay. The rural hotel Atzaró has a beach club here, or you can hire umbrellas and loungers right on the shore. During winter storms there's even some surf action.

Eating

Passion
CAFE €

10 Map p54, C5

This lovely cafe has a sea-facing terrace and a healthy eating menu that features predominantly vegetarian and raw food such as wild rice salad with butternut squash, feta and almonds (€13.50). It's perfect for breakfast, lunch or a light dinner. Or just grab a juice or smoothie (from €6.75), shake or protein punch. (☏971 80 73 23; http://passion-ibiza.com; Carrer Joan Tur Tur; meals €9-16.50; ⊙9am-11pm; 🛜🍴)

Croissant Show
CAFE €

11 Map p54, C4

The best butter-rich croissants and pastries in town, and their *café con leche* is perfectly made too. Enjoys a pedestrianised location, overlooking

---

Understand
Santa Eulària over the Years

There's some evidence of Roman settlement in the Santa Eulària region, and during the Moorish period its river valley was cleverly irrigated and intensively farmed – visit Can Planetes (p55) for more on this. But the town was still little more than an overgrown village until the 1930s, when American writer Elliot Paul spent an extended period here. He documented the town's Spanish Civil War years in his book *Life and Death of a Spanish Town*, a superb read. During the 1960s and 1970s the town became something of a hang-out for a British thespian set, centred on the popular bar Sandy's (now a Thai restaurant). Terry-Thomas and Denholm Elliott bought homes in the area, and Laurence Olivier, Elizabeth Taylor and John Mills holidayed in the town. Today Santa Eulària is a curious mix of summer holiday resort (complete with a smattering of British pubs) and a regular Spanish town.

Santa Eulària's mini-Ramblas. (☎971 31 96 10; Passeig de s'Alamera 5; snacks/light mains from €2/9; ☺8am-6pm; ☎)

El Bigotes
SEAFOOD €€

 12 Map p54, D1

This simple shoreside shack is known far and wide. There are two daily sittings: noon for grilled fish and 2pm for *bullit de peix* (fish stew simmered with herbs, mixed vegetables and potatoes). In July and August, turn up in person a couple of days before to book a spot, and be prepared to share a table. Food is €22 per person and the house wine is €10. Cash only. (Cala Mastella; meals €28-36; ☺noon-4pm Easter-Oct)

Es Terral
FRENCH, MEDITERRANEAN €€

13 Map p54, C4

A cut above the competition on Santa's street of restaurants, Es Terral imports many ingredients from France. It offers sublime seafood and fish – try the *bacalao al pil pil* (salt cod with garlic and hot peppers) – while standout meat dishes include crispy oxtail and duck rillette. It's run by a husband-and-wife team, with informed and attentive service. (☎628 581314; Carrer Sant Vicent 47; mains €12-22; ☺1-4pm & 7.30-11.45pm)

Can Pere
MEDITERRANEAN €€

14 Map p54, A4

This rural hotel has one of the most peaceful situations in Ibiza, on a hilltop with sweeping views over the wooded

Top Tip

Street of Restaurants
Just off the Plaça d'Espanya you'll find Santa Eulària's famous 'street of restaurants'. Pedestrianised Carrer Sant Vicent has over a dozen places to eat, from cafes and simple tapas joints to upmarket restaurants such as Es Terral.

centre of the island. Its restaurant offers fine Mediterranean cuisine, with expertly grilled meats and fresh seafood. It's 2km inland from Cala Llonga. (☎971 19 66 00; www.canpereibiza.com; mains €14-27; ☺8-11.30pm May-Oct; ☎)

La Noria
SEAFOOD €€

15 Map p54, D1

Offering a fine outlook from its terrace over the Mediterranean, this popular restaurant is renowned for its seafood, with excellent paella (around €40 for two; order ahead), *bullit de peix* and grilled fish. They also offer Ibizan wines. (☎971 33 53 97; Cala Boix; ☺1-4pm & 7-11pm May-Sep, 1-4pm Sat-Sun Oct-Apr)

El Bacaro
ITALIAN, PIZZA €€

16 Map p54, D4

Reliable, welcoming Italian in the marina district that offers the best pizza and calzone in town, good seafood and pasta and a few regional dishes from Venice, the owner's home town. (☎971 33 19 43; Carrer Isidor Macabich 35; mains €12-20; ☺1pm-midnight Mar–mid-Jan)

Local Life
Can Cosmi

Can Cosmi (971 80 73 15; Carrer San
Jamie 44; meals €9-18; 8am–1am) is
a long-running, no-nonsense place
that serves inexpensive tapas (most
€2.50 to €3.50) all day and ice-
cold draught beer. It is said to have
created the famous Ibiza *tostada*
(toasted baguette with ripe tomato
topping). Their meal deal (€12) includes three tapas, bread and aioli,
olives, dessert and a coffee.

El Naranjo   SEAFOOD €€

17   Map p54, C4

Hidden away from the bustle, 'The
Orange Tree' has a pretty courtyard
draped in bougainvillea. The fish (such
as sea bass in a salt crust) is always
fresh and cooked to retain all its juices.
The *menú del día* (€10) is a steal.
(971 33 03 24; Carrer Sant Josep 31; mains
€10-18; 1-4pm & 7pm-midnight Tue-Sun;)

Ses Savines   INTERNATIONAL €€

18   Map p54, B3

This slick, seafront lounge-restaurant
has sofas and loungers for drinking
in the stunning views. Go for drinks,
snacks (goat's cheese salad, baguettes)
or Med-meets-Asia mains like cod loin
in a soy reduction with tempura vegetables. There's live jazz on Tuesdays
and Thursdays in the summer. (971
33 18 24; Cala ses Estaques; snacks €5-10,
mains €12-34; noon-midnight late Apr-Oct)

Amante   MEDITERRANEAN €€€

19   Map p54, A4

On a remote cove beach, Amante
has a spectacular, secluded location
overlooking the Med and attracts a hip
crowd. During the day it's more of a
'beach club' (read pricey sun lounges)
but from around sunset it's a fine place
to dine with a creative, if expensive,
Spanish and Italian menu. The bar
stays open till 2am, and Amante hosts
some great one-off events with DJs and
dancing under the stars. (971 19 61 76;
www.amanteibiza.com; Sol d'en Serra; mains
€17-33; 11am-midnight May-early Oct;)

Drinking

Babylon Beach Ibiza   BAR

20   Map p54, B3

With tables by the waves and cool vibes
on the stereo, this groovy beach joint is
the best lounge-around bar-resto on the
East Coast. They serve good grub, with
organic ingredients, including Sunday
roasts. It's just off the coastal road.
(971 33 21 81; www.babylonbeachbar.com;
10am-midnight Apr-Oct;)

Jam Shack   BAR

21   Map p54, A4

Just off the beach in Cala Llonga (5km
south of Santa Eulària), this lively joint
is owned by a British/Jamaican couple
and offers rum punch, cocktails and
great tunes (reggae, funk and soul). On
Thursdays the Jamaican BBQ features
jerk chicken, coconut-steamed fish and

Passeig de s'Alamera (p55)

Antoni circuit. Good local DJs man the decks, spinning deep house, and there's live music on Sunday evenings. (www.guaranaibiza.com; Passeig Marítim; ⏱8pm-6am May-Oct)

Shopping

Queens of Joy Fashion CLOTHING

24 🔒 Map p54, C4

Santa Eulària's best boutique stocks flowing and fitted dresses in silk and cotton, stylish bags, hats by designer Berri Shulman-Hill, Ibiza Soul flip-flops and quirky jewellery. (✆971 80 78 78; Carrer Mariano Riquer Wallis; ⏱10.30am-2pm & 5.30-9.30pm Mon-Sat, 6-10pm Sun)

Polen FOOD & DRINK

25 🔒 Map p54, D4

This deli sells all kinds of gourmet produce from Ibiza, including honey and salt, as well as fair trade and organic foodstuffs such as granola and wine. (✆634 843374; Carrer Sant Llorenç 14; ⏱9.30am-7pm Mon-Sat)

Octopus CHILDREN, CLOTHING

26 🔒 Map p54, D4

Sells lots of unusual and good-quality toys and games for kids as well as quirky presents (bags, hats) for adults. Many things are sustainably produced. (✆971 80 74 92; octopusshopibiza.blogspot.com.es; Carrer Sant Llorenç 22; ⏱10.30am-1.45pm & 5-8.30pm Mon-Sat)

rice 'n' peas. (✆636 013098; Carrer Monte Aconcagua, Cala Llonga; ⏱noon-1am May-Oct)

Royalty BAR

22 🍸 Map p54, C4

This drinking institution enjoys a prime corner plot in the town centre and is a superb spot to nurse a beer or sip a coffee and watch the world go by. Prices are very moderate, and they serve food too. (Carrer Sant Jaume 51; ⏱8am-1.30am)

Guaraná CLUB

23 🍸 Map p54, D4

By the marina, this is a cool club away from the Ibiza Town–Sant Rafel–Sant

Explore

Northern Ibiza

The least populated and most rustic part of the island, northern Ibiza has a boho, off-grid vibe thanks to its hippy heritage. Package tourism and clubbing have minimal impact here. There are few conventional sights, but it's a wonderful region to explore with whitewashed villages, forested hills and a craggy coastline blessed with some stunning cove beaches. Sant Joan offers a slice of low-key Ibizan life, while Portinatx is the area's busiest resort.

The Region in a Day

Begin in tranquil Sant Carles with breakfast at **Anita's** (p80). Check out the village **church** (p63), then cruise up to Portinatx for a morning hike to its lonely lighthouse.

Then hit the beach at either Cala d'en Serra (p65), **Benirràs** (p65) or **Aigües Blanques** (p65). Lunch by the shore (all these beaches have places offering fresh seafood) then don a mask and snorkel and check out underwater Ibiza – visibility often tops 30m. In the late afternoon drop by chic hotel **Atzaró** (p142) for a drink and perhaps indulge in a spa treatment, if funds permit.

In the evening head for Santa Gertrudis, where there's a choice of restaurants and bars to enjoy, a quirky auction house and plenty of boutiques for treats. Or for one of the island's best dining experiences, make for **La Paloma** (p77) in Sant Llorenç, where you can dine on creative mod-Med cuisine on the lovely terrace. There are no clubs in the north, but bar-cum-hippy hang-out **Las Dalias** (p81) often has live music.

For a local's day in Santa Gertrudis, see p66 and for a local's day experiencing off-the-beaten-track coves, see p68.

Top Experiences

Local Life

Best of Northern Ibiza

Eating

Villages

Getting There

Bus L20 Ibiza Town–Sant Llorenç–Sant Joan (Mon–Fri, four daily, Sat & Sun, one to two daily).

Bus 25 Ibiza Town–Santa Gertrudis–Sant Miquel (Mon–Sat eight to nine daily May–Oct, reduced service in winter).

Top Experiences
Sant Carles de Peralta

A quiet, unhurried village that has been attracting bohemian travellers since the 1960s, Sant Carles de Peralta is surrounded by rolling hills and is close to wonderful beaches. Lead was mined in the region from Roman times until the early 20th century, but today it's tourism that fires the local economy.

◉ Map p70, D3

Getting There

🚌 **Bus** L16 connects Sant Carles with Santa Eulària (five daily Mon–Fri May–Oct, nine buses Sat, no buses Sun). Reduced service in winter.

Església de Sant Carles

Don't Miss

Església de Sant Carles

Sant Carles' village **church** is a striking 18th-century building, with an impressive arcaded entrance porch and a simple interior with a single nave. Today's peaceful scene belies a traumatic past, for in 1936, during the Spanish Civil War, Republican forces hung both the village priest and his father from the carob tree (which still stands outside the church). The Republicans and the Catholic Church were on separate sides during the war and in author Elliot Paul's account of the incident, he attests that the father and son were killed after taking shots at Republican troops from the belfry.

Es Trui de Ca'n Andreu

Seventeenth-century **Es Trui de Ca'n Andreu** (Map p70, E3; admission €3; ⏱10.30am-2pm & 3.30-5pm Sat) is a fine example of an Ibizan *casament* (farmhouse), a cubist structure of blinding white walls, tiny windows and low, timbered roofs. 'Es trui' refers to the house's massive olive press, which you'll find in the traditional kitchen. Ibizan farming tools, musical instruments and handmade baskets are also exhibited, and local wine and *hierbas* liquor are available for purchase.

Nearby: Torre d'en Valls

With majestic views over the Mediterranean from a patch of volcanic rock, the 17th-century **Torre d'en Valls** (Map p70, E3) is one of the island's best-preserved defence towers. Ibiza's towers would have been manned night and day, and if pirates were sighted a horn was sounded or a fire lit, so islanders knew to take refuge. From this tower you get a terrific perspective of the offshore islet of Tagomago.

☑ **Top Tips**

▸ Bring your swimming gear. There are several spectacular beaches near Sant Carles including tiny Cala d'en Serra.

▸ Saturdays are always very busy in Sant Carles, with a huge market at Las Dalias (p81).

✗ **Take a Break**

An essential stop in Sant Carles, Anita's (p80) is one of the original hippy watering holes (the art on the walls is said to have been donated to clear bar tabs). While you're here, be sure to try the local *hierbas* liquor. For grilled meats, rustic Cas Pagès (p77) offers inexpensive and authentic Ibiza country cooking.

Top Experiences
Northern Beaches

Ibiza has over 30 coves, and the northern beaches of Cala d'en Serra, Benirràs and Aigües Blanques are three of the very best. Each has its own allure: Cala d'en Serra is (just) accessible by car, but still feels like a real discovery; Benirràs has had a distinctly hippy identity since the 1960s when it was the destination for wild happenings; and nudist Aigües Blanques is the place in the north to head for a Balearic sunrise.

◉ Map p70

Getting There

🚌 **Bus** No buses serve Benirràs or Cala d'en Serra. Santa Eulària–Cala de Sant Vicent buses (three daily Jun–Sep only) pass Aigües Blanques; check www.ibizabus.com.

Benirràs

Don't Miss

Cala d'en Serra

This exquisite little **bay** (Map p70, D1), around 3km east of Portinatx, has to be one of the most beautiful on the island. The approach road to the beach is truly spectacular, offering a succession of vistas over azure water far below, though it is very rough and potholed. Once you reach the shore there's a tiny sandy beach, a collection of fisher's shacks, and an excellent Dutch-run **chiringuito** (Cala d'en Serra; snacks €6, meals €12-16; ☉10am-9pm May-Oct) for very moderately priced snacks and drinks.

Benirràs

Reached via a spectacular serpentine road, the virtually untouched sandy bay of **Benirràs** (Map p70, C2) has high, forested cliffs and a trio of bar-restaurants. It's a spectacular location for sunsets, a location Ibiza's boho tribe have favoured for decades. If you visit on a Sunday there's always an assembly of drummers banging out a salutation to the sun.

The curiously shaped offshore island at the mouth of the bay is **Cap Bernat** – it's said to resemble a praying nun, the Carthaginian goddess Tanit, or even the Sphinx.

Aigües Blanques

Facing east, the exposed beach of **Aigües Blanques** (White Waters; Map p70, E2) gets its name from the surf which can whip up here when there are strong winds. Most of the year things are actually very tranquil, and the scenery is stunning, with sandy bays divided by crumbling cliffs. This is an officially designated nudist beach, and very popular with North Ibiza's hippy community. It's also the perfect spot to witness a sunrise over the Med, and has a good **chiringuito** (snacks €6, meals from €10; ☉10am-10pm Easter-Nov).

☑ Top Tips

▶ Benirràs gets very busy on Sundays; arrive early to get a parking place.

▶ Sun-worshippers (or shade-seekers) note that the high cliffs behind Aigües Blanques cast a shadow over the beach in the late afternoon.

▶ The dirt track down to Cala d'en Serra is in very poor condition. Consider parking at the top and hiking down, unless you have a high clearance vehicle.

✕ Take a Break

Cala d'en Serra's *chiringuito* is a good-value place offering cheap baguettes, full meals, draught beer, wine and juices. Benirràs has a choice of three places to eat. Aigües Blanques' *chiringuito*, at the southern end of the beach, is inexpensive and always popular.

Local Life
Hanging Out in Santa Gertrudis

Blink and you might miss tiny Santa Gertrudis de Fruitera. This once sleepy, whitewashed village at the island's heart is a gem. You'll find craft galleries, an auction house and a bookshop, plus several good cafes and bars around the central, pedestrianised Plaça de l'Església. For such a pipsqueak of a village, Santa Gertrudis also has some terrific restaurants.

❶ Start the Day

Musset (www.mussetibiza.com; Carrer Venda de Sa Picassa Bajos; meals €8-15; ☺9am-11pm; ☎) is a chic cafe-restaurant, with inviting decor and furnishings (check out its glass floor, which showcases a terracotta seabed sculpture), and a great front terrace. Excellent à la carte breakfast options (served until 2pm) include pancakes, omelettes, fine fresh juices and pastries. The three-course set menu (€14.95) features healthy eating options.

❷ Village Church

Overlooking the central square, the 18th-century **Església de Santa Gertrudis** (Plaça de l'Església) has an imposing whitewashed facade, its small windows picked out with yellow paint. The largely sombre interior is embellished with a few decorative touches including oranges and figs, a nod to Santa Gertrudis' status as Ibiza's principal fruit-growing village.

❸ Morning Workout

The professional, well-equipped **Pilates Studio** (www.pilatestudioibiza.com; Calle Venda de Llatzer 11; classes from €12; ☉9am-9pm Mon-Fri, 10am-2pm Sat) teaches the Stott Pilates method. Experienced instructors use mat work, reformer machines, the 'tower' and the 'chair'. Personal trainers are also available for redcord and weights workouts. Book ahead.

❹ Healthy Lunch

Wild Beets (📞971 19 78 70; wildbeets.com; Carrer Venda de Llatzer 15; mains €9.50-14.50; ☉9am-11pm; 🛜🌱) offers a terrific menu of creative vegan dishes, with lots of raw food options. Salads are excellent – try *ensalada super food* (with young green leaves, avocado and nuts). There are kids' dishes (all €7.50), too. The airy, stylish premises, with shared bench seating, adds to its appeal.

❺ Browse Some Books

A little west of the centre, the inviting **Libro Azul** (www.libro-azul-ibiza.com; Carrer Venda de Parada 21; ☉10.30am-2pm & 5-8pm Mon-Fri, 10.30am-2pm Sat) bookshop always has a good stock of titles about Ibiza's culture, nature and history as well as art and design books, photographic titles and literature in several languages. They regularly host readings and book launches here.

❻ Going...Going...Gone

The quirky auction house **Casi Todo** (📞971 19 70 23; www.casitodo.com; ☉10am-2pm & 6-10pm Jun-Sep, shorter hours in winter) is a treat to browse, with everything from classic cars to gypsy carts, 1920s jewellery and 1970s costumes going under the hammer every two to three weeks. Check its website for the next event and an online catalogue.

❼ Evening Drink

Santa Gertrudis' most famous bar is **Bar Costa** (Plaça de l'Església 11; snacks/meals from €3/9; ☉8am-1am), with original paintings plastered on every wall of its cavernous interior. It's great for a casual drink, with a large outdoor terrace and an interior far larger than its frontage would suggest.

❽ Dine in Style

Undoubtedly one of Ibiza's best Italian restaurants, **Macao Cafe** (📞971 19 78 35; Venda des Pobles 8; mains €17-35; ☉7.30pm-midnight Apr-Sep; 🛜) has a gorgeous tree-shaded terrace that comes into its own during the summer months, and a modish interior. It's expensive, but given the quality of the food and dining experience, it's worth it. Pasta dishes, fish (try the tuna *scottata* with tomato and baby salad leaves) and meat are all sublime.

Local Life
Off-the-Beaten-Track Coves

Even in the peak of high season, some of the coves dotted across Northern Ibiza are nearly deserted. Most of these spots require a little effort to get to; you'll often have to park your car and walk a while to get to them. Your reward is a sense of isolation, with just the majesty of the coastal landscape to marvel at.

❶ Pou des Lleó

Pou des Lleó is a small pebble-and-sand bay ringed by red cliffs and fishing huts around 5km east of Sant Carles. During the summer months (late May to September) there's a *chiringuito* for snacks and drinks. You'll also find the restaurant **Salvador** (Map p70, E3; ☎971 18 78 79; Pou des Lleó; meals €16-32; ⏱1-3.30pm & 7.30-11.30pm daily Apr-Oct, open weekends only in winter) here, which specialises in seafood. You can drive right up to the shore.

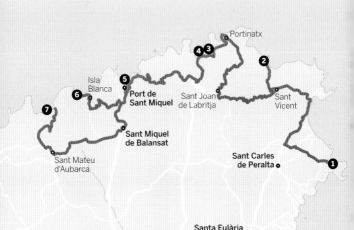

2 Port de ses Caletes

From the tiny village of Sant Vicent a steep, twisting road ascends a hillside before plunging to a remote pebbly cove, less than 100m across, where there's a scattering of dilapidated fisher's huts. Coastal cliffs soar above the bay. For solitude and silence, Port de ses Caletes can't be beat.

3 Cala Xuclar

This lovely sheltered beach is 500m from the Sant Joan–Portinatx road, at the end of a dusty dirt track. Once you reach the shore its turquoise waters dazzle the eyes – bring snorkelling gear, for the water is fabulously clear. Just back from the shore, **Chiringuito Cala Xuclar** (Map p70, D1; ☑607 233019; Cala Xuclar; meals €18-32; ☺11am-10pm May-Sep) is excellent for seafood.

4 s'Illot des Renclí

Between Calas Xuclar and Xarraca, just a few metres north of the coastal road, is the tiny cove of **s'Illot des Renclí**. Here there's an inviting patch of sand, shallow, pellucid water perfect for swimming, and a well-regarded seafood restaurant. Just offshore is s'*Illot* (the Islet), after which the beach is named.

5 Cala des Moltons

This little *cala* is just 250m from the resort of Port de Sant Miquel; simply follow the path to the west around the bay. **Cala des Moltons** has a tiny sandy beach, wonderfully sheltered swimming and the superb **Chiringuito Utopía** (Cala des Moltons; meals €10-15; ☺10am-10pm May-Sep). Continue along the same trail for another kilometre and you'll reach the Torre des Molar defence tower.

6 Portitxol

Encircled by a necklace of cliffs, this tiny, lonely and very isolated horse-shoe-shaped rocky **cove** is perfect if you need to escape the world for an afternoon. Most of the year there's no one here, except the odd fisher (their huts fringe the back of the bay). It's a 20-minute walk west of Isla Blanca.

7 Cala d'Aubarca

The giant bite-shaped bay of **Cala d'Aubarca** is around 3km across – its sheer scale can't fail to impress. It's 4km north of the village Sant Mateu, from where a rough dirt track leads up to wooded cliffs high above the bay. There's no beach; you'll have to park up and hike down to the shoreline (it's around 20 minutes).

Cova de Can Marçà

Experiences

Església de Sant Miquel CHURCH

1 ⊙ Map p70, B2

Sant Miquel de Balansat is not a picture-postcard village – its streets are lined with apartment blocks – but its little hillock (once a refuge from pirates) is graced by a shimmering white 14th-century fortress church. The restored early- 17th-century frescoes in the Capella de Benirràs are a swirl of flowers and twisting vines. Each Thursday from June to September, there's traditional island dancing on the pretty patio at 6.15pm. (⊙9.30am-1.30pm & 4.30-7.30pm Tue-Fri, 9.30am-12.30pm Sat)

Cova de Can Marçà CAVE

2 ⊙ Map p70, B2

A turn-off on the east just before Port de Sant Miquel takes you around a headland to these underground caverns (once a smugglers' hideaway) which are spectacularly lit by coloured lights. Tours in various languages take around 30 minutes. After resurfacing, pause for a drink on its terrace and savour the panorama of sheer cliffs and deep blue water. (www.covadecanmarsa. com; adult/child €10.50/6.50; ⊙10.30am-1.30pm & 2.30-8pm May-Oct, 11am-5.30pm Nov-Apr)

Portinatx

Santa Agnès de Corona VILLAGE

3 ⊙ Map p70, A3

Tiny Santa Agnès de Corona is centred around a rustic church, which dates from 1806, and boasts an excellent ethnographic museum, **Es Pujol** (☏696 630443; admission free; ⊙11am-7pm Mon-Fri). The village is surrounded by thousands of almond trees, which blossom in late January and early February, filling the plain with pink-white blossom, a spectacular sight.

Cala de Sant Vicent BEACH

4 ⊙ Map p70, E2

The package-tour resort of Cala de Sant Vicent extends around the shores of a protected bay on the northeast coast. Its long stretch of sandy beach is backed by a string of modern mid-rise hotels. A 2.5km drive northwards winds through a leafy residential area high up to Punta Grossa, with spectacular views over the coast and east out to sea.

Portinatx
BEACH

5 ⊙ Map p70, D1

Portinatx is the north coast's major tourist resort. Busy, yes, but a good spot for families and positively underpopulated when set against the megaresorts further south. Its three adjoining beaches – S'Arenal Petit, S'Arenal Gran and Platja Es Port – are each beautiful but often crowded.

Port de Sant Miquel
BEACH

6 ⊙ Map p70, B2

A former fishing village, Port de Sant Miquel is now a busy resort, with a fine beach dominated by the huge concrete honeycomb of Hotel Club San Miguel. In this attractive, deep-sunk bay, you can waterski, canoe and hire snorkelling gear to explore the rocky shoreline. Offshore, the tiny island Illa des Bosc boasts a stunning villa that enjoys its own private beach.

Església de Sant Llorenç
CHURCH

7 ⊙ Map p70, C3

The quiet hamlet of Sant Llorenç has a brilliant-white 18th-century fortress-church, built at time when attacks by Moorish pirates were the scourge of the island. The church boasts a broad entrance porch while its nave has an attractive barrel-vaulted roof. Do check out the excellent cafe-restaurant La Paloma (p77) while you're here.

○ Local Life
Cova des Cuieram

You'll have to use your imagination to appreciate this modest-looking cave. Consisting of a few small chambers, it isn't visually impressive, but it does form a vital part of Ibiza's cultural legacy. **Cova des Cuieram** (☾9.30am-1.30pm Tue-Sat) was an important Carthaginian place of worship; around 600 terracotta images of the fertility goddess Tanit have been found here. You can see some in Ibiza Town's Necròpolis del Puig des Molins (p38). Reflecting Ibiza's hippy-spiritual side, many visitors leave offerings to Tanit.

The cave is located in one of the remotest corners of the island, 2km north of Cala de Sant Vicent; the signposted turn-off is north of the Sant Vicent–Cala de Sant Vicent road. The access road is paved, but you'll have to walk the last few hundred metres.

Església de Sant Mateu d'Aubarca
CHURCH

8 ⊙ Map p70, A3

Tiny Sant Mateu d'Aubarca is one of the most isolated villages in Ibiza, the focus of the region's farming community (there are several local vineyards). It's worth dropping by its fortified church, which dates from the late 18th century, and has a triple-arched front porch and two tiny chapels. 'Aubarca' refers to a nearby bay, once the village's port.

Local Life
Hiking to Portinatx Lighthouse

There are many lighthouses dotted around the coast of the Balearic Islands, and this majestic structure is the largest; its lantern is 2.25m in diameter. From Portinatx's Platja Es Port (where there's parking), there's a beautiful waymarked trail to the **lighthouse** (Far de Portinatx; Map p70, D1). The path follows the rugged coastal cliffs high above the sea, dipping down past rocky bays and through patches of pine forest. Southern Mallorca is visible on clear days. Allow an hour (in total) to make it there and back to Portinatx.

Balàfia
VILLAGE

 9 Map p70, C3

Take a lane off the C733 highway beside the restaurant **Camí de Balàfia** (☏ 971 32 50 19; Carretera Sant Joan Km 15.4; meals €18-25; ⊙ 8-11.30pm Mon-Sat) to reach the minuscule, once-fortified hamlet of Balàfia, where several homes have their own defence towers. Balàfia is sometimes described as an Arab village, though the only thing definitely Arabic about the settlement is its name. There are lots of *privado* signs around – but don't let these deter you from exploring its couple of lanes.

Figueral
BEACH

 10 Map p70, E3

This slender 200m beach of dark sand is swept clean by foaming waves, and there's some surf here when a strong northeasterly blows. A scattering of hotels and villas are dotted around Figueral, which attracts a well-heeled clientele of French and German families. In terms of ambience it feels a million miles away from the boisterous, British-geared resorts elsewhere.

Eating

Can Cosmi
IBIZAN €

Tiny, isolated Santa Agnès (see 3 Map p70, A3) is little more than a cluster of houses around a church but it does have a terrific bar-restaurant that's famous above all for its fabulous *tortilla* (Spanish omelette). It also sells meat dishes including tasty grilled chicken. (light meals €6-12; ⊙ 11.30am-11pm Wed-Mon)

Giri Café
CAFE €€

11 Map p70, D2

A stunning cafe-restaurant, which ticks all the right progressive foodie boxes – declaring it uses seasonal, locally sourced, sustainably produced and (mainly) organic ingredients. But does Giri deliver? Yes, it does. The cuisine is imaginatively cooked and presented and the interior and garden are sublime. Specials might include cod au gratin with soft garlic, hummus and red onion salad (€19).

Drop by for a casual coffee or juice (try the antioxidant with red fruit and orange juice). The building itself is worthy of mention too; it's a designer's delight complete with sandstone walls and a modish conservatory, while the rear garden with Bali-style day beds borders fields. (☏ 971 33 34 74; www.cafe. thegiri.com; Plaça Espanya 5, Sant Joan; mains €14-22; ⊙ 10am-midnight; 🛜)

Chiringuito Cala Xuclar

SEAFOOD €€

 Map p70, D1

Well hidden from the north coast road, this delightful little *chiringuito* (beach shack) offers some of the freshest fish in Ibiza, including grouper, monkfish and John Dory. The situation really is idyllic, at the back of a remote cove beach, but the place is tiny and space limited. Text a day or two in advance to book a table. (☏ 607 233019; Cala Xuclar; meals €18-32; ⊙ 11am-10pm May-Sep)

Top Tip

Es Amunts

The densely forested Es Amunts hills, which run in an arc between Cala Salada and Sant Carles, form the north's largest range, covering 15,000 hectares (a quarter of the island). You can learn about the region's culture and environment in the **Centre d'interpretació Es Amunts** (☏ 971 32 51 41; esamunts. caib.es; admission free; ⊙ 9am-2pm Wed), a modern interpretation facility in the village of Sant Llorenç; note it's only open on Wednesdays.

Ses Escoles

IBIZAN €€

 Map p70, C4

This olive oil estate has a delightful cafe-restaurant which offers Ibizan cheeses and meats, tapas and canapes and some good dishes for vegetarians (try the *parrillada variada de verduras*). The premises are historic (it's an old school building) and atmospheric. Book ahead on weekends, and be sure to check out the deli, too. (☏ 971 87 02 29; www.canmiquelguasch; Ctra Ibiza Town–Sant Joan Km 9.2; mains €10-20; ⊙ 8.30am-1am)

Can Caus

IBIZAN €€

 Map p70, B4

An excellent place that sources most of its produce from the island. It's renowned for grilled meats – goat, lamb, *sobrassada* (paprika and other spices) and *butifarra* (blood) sausages – which are grilled to perfection. Ibizan cheeses, wines and desserts are also available. The atmosphere is gregarious, with tables set under a covered terrace. (☏ 971 19 75 16; cancaus-ibiza.es; Ctra Ibiza Town–Santa Gertrudis Km 3.5; meals €16-24; ⊙ noon-midnight daily Apr-Sep, closed Mon Oct-May)

Es Caliu

IBIZAN €€

 Map p70, C4

A rustic restaurant, centred around an old farmhouse, that specialises in grilled meat (and nothing else). Try the leg of lamb or *entrecotte a la*

Understand

Ibizan Wine

Ibiza's arid climate is not ideal for intensive viniculture, but there are vineyards producing high-quality wines, concentrated in the northwest around the village of Sant Mateu d'Aubarca. Richly aromatic local reds, including earthy monastrell and spicy garnacha (grenache), are favoured, along with some tempranillo, merlot and syrah. Malvasía is the main variety for whites and rosés.

Ibiza's leading wineries include the award-winning **Can Rich** (☑971 80 33 77; www.bodegascanrich.com; Camí de Sa Vorera) in the Buscastell area (east of Sant Antoni), with 21 hectares planted with seven different grapes. The winery offers tastings (with tapas) and brief tours (book ahead). **Sa Cova** (☑971 18 70 46; www.sacovaibiza.com) in Sant Mateu is another important producer, and well worth visiting for tastings and its restaurant. North of Sant Rafel, **Ibizkus** (☑695 258148; www.ibizkus.com; Camí Vell de Sant Mateu; ⊙tours 10am-2pm Mon-Fri) makes premium rosés (40,000 bottles per year) and a few reds from old, organically cultivated and largely ungrafted vines; tours can be arranged. **Can Maymó** (www.bodegascanmaymo.com) in Sant Mateu is another notable winery. In addition, most Ibizan farmers cultivate a few *parras* (vines) to produce some *vi pagès* (country wine) for casual drinking.

Wine Festival

If you're in Ibiza in December, you can't miss the terrific annual wine harvest festival in Sant Mateu d'Aubarca, which celebrates the local *vi pagès*. Everyone samples the vintage from teapot-shaped glass jugs called *porros,* and there's much munching of *sobrassada* (paprika) and *butifarra* (blood) sausages.

Stockists

Local shops, supermarkets and many restaurants offer Ibizan wine. As island wineries are much smaller than those on the mainland, they don't have the same economies of scale. Expect to pay a little more than you would for a basic bottle of Spanish plonk – from around €6. Vino y Co (p113) is an excellent wine merchant which has good supplies of Ibizan wines, often available for tasting. You'll find it on the Ibiza Town–Sant Josep road at Km 1.6.

pimienta verde y Roquefort (steak with peppercorns and blue cheese). There's a pleasant terrace for the summer months. (☏971 32 50 75; www.escaliuibiza. com; Ctra Ibiza Town–Sant Joan Km 10.8; meals €15-28; ⏲7.30pm-midnight Jul-Aug, 1-3.30pm & 7.30-11.30pm Sep-Jun)

Cas Pagès
BARBECUE, IBIZAN €€

16 Map p70, D4

Very popular with locals, this casual fine-country restaurant special- ises in barbecued meats – succulent pork steaks, tasty lamb chops and beef – all well seasoned with Ibiza salt. Portions are huge; if you're not desper- ately hungry you may find one plate will suffice for two. There's a lovely vine-shaded terrace and rustic interior. No reservations. (caspages.es; Ctra Sta Eulària–Sant Carles Km 10; meals €13-25; ⏲1-3.30pm & 7.30-11.30pm Wed-Mon)

Salvador
SEAFOOD €€

17 Map p70, E3

Located on a tiny bay 5km east of Sant Carles, this seafood restaurant serves superb *bullit de peix* (fish stew sim- mered with herbs, mixed vegetables and potatoes) which is served with with *arròs a banda* (paella-style rice cooked in fish stock). Grilled fish, squid and cuttlefish are also available. Tables overlook the water. (☏971 18 78 79; Pou des Lleó; meals €16-32; ⏲1-3.30pm & 7.30-11.30pm daily Apr-Oct, open weekends only in winter)

 Top Tip

Chiringuito Utopía
Chiringuito Utopía (Cala des Moltons; meals €10-15; ⏲10am-10pm May-Sep) is a very stylish, inviting beach shack at the rear of Cala des Moltons, a tiny sandy bay just steps west of Port de Sant Miquel. Beauti- fully prepared meals are offered and there's a fab-value *sardinada* (sardine barbecue), costing €11 per person on Fridays and Saturdays. Impromptu live music events are held here, and you'll find Bali-style daybeds for lounging.

Es Pins
IBIZAN €€

18 Map p70, C3

Classic, no-nonsense Ibizan restau- rant with very inexpensive prices and a straightforward menu. It's very old school – portions are huge and the decor is log-cabin homely – and that's just the way the local farmers like it. *Sofrit pagès* (country fry-up of meats) is the house special, or order the rabbit (€15) or pork chops (€10). Bread is baked in house and the *aioli* is homemade. (☏971 32 50 34; Ctra Ibiza Town–Sant Joan Km 12; meals €14-24; ⏲1- 4pm & 7.30-11.30pm, closed Wed)

La Paloma
MEDITERRANEAN €€€

19 Map p70, C3

There's a mellow vibe at this boho-cool restaurant set in lush gardens, 100m

Understand

Hippy Heritage

The north of Ibiza has been a focus for the island's hippies since the mid-1960s. With cheap farmhouses available for rent and tolerant locals, many settled in the area. Mail and cheques could be collected at Anita's bar in Sant Carles, and their ranks were boosted by American draft-dodgers fleeing the Vietnam War. The film *More,* which deals with heroin addiction and has a soundtrack by Pink Floyd, was filmed on the island in 1969. Later a scene developed around the Can Tiruit commune near Sant Joan, which became a centre for the charismatic Indian guru Bhagwan Rajneesh (later known as Osho). Osho preached a mix of sexual liberation, Sufism and Buddhism to thousands of mainly Western devotees (and combined it with a love of Rolls-Royces). Ibiza folklore has it that Osho followers were the first people to bring MDMA to the island in the late 1970s.

Hippy heritage is everywhere across the north. At nudist beach Aigües Blanques there's a startling vista of the island of Tagomago, celebrated in an album by psychedelic rockers Can. Benirràs beach is also steeped in countercultural history. Full moon parties were held here for decades, and during the build up to the Gulf War in 1991 thousands gathered to protest. The bay reverberated to the rhythmic beat of the conga and bongo, an event later dubbed the **Day of the Drums**. Today you can get a flavour of this occasion each Sunday when dozens of drummers gather at Benirràs to mark the setting of the sun.

The energy and psychedelic edge (and drugs) of the Acid House scene resonated strongly in northern Ibiza, where few identified with the expense and glitz of Ibiza's superclubs. An underground trance movement developed in the 1990s, with organisers setting up PAs in remote rural locations. Key venues across the north included the Portinatx lighthouse, Can Punta hilltop, and Las Puertas del Cielo, near Santa Agnès, where a three-day party was held in 1999. But as these illegal raves were increasingly targeted by the authorities the scene dissipated; legal venues such as Las Dalias (p81) have stepped in to host psy-trance parties.

Sardinada (sardine barbecue)

downhill from the church. The food is mod-Med with a creative slant – herby salads with garden veg, homemade focaccia, Tuscan antipasti and terrific lamb chops marinated in soy sauce and honey. The cafe serves great quiches, carrot cake and organic smoothies on its shady, overgrown terrace. (🕽971 32 55 43; mains €16-28; 🕑cafe 10.30am-4.30pm year-round, restaurant 7.30-11.30pm Mar-Oct; 🛜👪)

Ama Lur
BASQUE €€€

20 🍴 Map p70, C4

One of the best-regarded restaurants on the island, Ama Lur often wins the Ibiza chefs' own annual 'Top Restaurant' award. It's quite formal and proper with exquisite Basque cuisine that includes

plenty of fish and seafood and an extensive, if expensive wine list. The staff and management go the extra mile in terms of service. (🕽971 31 45 54; www.restaurante amalur.com; Ctra Ibiza Town–Sant Miquel Km 2.3; meals €28-52; 🕑noon-4pm & 8pm-12.30am)

Top Tip

Market Day

Sant Joan hosts one of the most authentic farmers markets in Ibiza (each Sunday from 10.30am) with stalls selling organic local produce along with traditional crafts and handicrafts. There's often a live band and always a lively, sociable atmosphere.

Local Life

Sant Joan

Delightful little **Sant Joan de Labritja** (Map p70, D2) contains no more than a few hundred residents, but it is one of the principal settlements in the north of the island (and a municipal capital). Along its charming little high street you'll find a cluster of shops, some venerable whitewashed cottages and a couple of good cafe-restaurants, including the superb Giri Café. Geographically isolated from the capital, Sant Joan's rustic character has made it a popular base for writers, artists and escapees from the rat race. Counterculture is virtually mainstream here, and the town has long played host to esoteric types, from the days of the Bhagwan Rajneesh cult back in the 1970s.

The only real sight in the village is the **Església de Sant Joan**, a typically Ibizan whitewashed 18th-century construction with the slightly unusual addition of a slim steeple that dates from the 20th century. The interior is very plain, its nave topped with a barrel-vaulted roof.

Try to drop by on a Sunday when there's an excellent local market in the village centre.

Drinking

Anita's

BAR

A timeless tavern opposite the village church in Sant Carles de Peralta (Map p70, D3), Anita's has been attracting all sorts since the hippies rocked up here in the 1960s. The kitchen churns out great tapas, pizza and mains like roast pork and chicken– or simply to drink and chat. You must try the homemade *hierbas* liquor, a blend of 16 ingredients including rosemary, fennel, orange and lemon. (☺7am-1am)

Cafe Vista Alegre

CAFE

21 Map p70, D2

With a lovely front terrace that catches the morning sun, this local's local is ideal for a *café con leche* (milky coffee) early in the day or a cheeky beer later in the afternoon. On Wednesdays it prepares an excellent *bullit de peix* and Ibizan classics like *tostadas* and *flaó* are always available. (☎971 33 30 08; Carrer Eivissa 1, Sant Joan; snacks/meals from €4/9; ☺8am-1am)

Zulu Lounge

LOUNGE

For good chill-out tunes and a vista of the bay, this little bar-restaurant is your best bet in Portinatx (see 5 ☺ Map p70, D1). There's an extensive cocktail list, and some Mexican and Spanish dishes on the menu. (S'Arenal Petit; ☺noon-1am May-Oct)

Hippy market at Las Dalias

Entertainment

Las Dalias

LIVE MUSIC

22 Map p70, D3

One-size-fits-all venue that caters to North Ibiza's alternative crew with psy-trance nights, live music (everything from blues to Afrobeat and reggae; Manu Chao played here in 2015). DJ events include Waxda Jam for funk, hip-hop and bass sounds. There's a lively bar, restaurant, and Las Dalias also hosts a huge Saturday hippy market. (971 32 68 25; www.lasdalias.es; 8am-2am, later for events;)

Shopping

Oleoteca Ses Escoles

FOOD & DRINK

This beautiful deli-temple is primarily concerned with gourmet olive oil. Its house brand is organic, extra virgin and made in Ibiza (you can taste it before you buy). It also stocks Ibiza wine and liquor, natural perfumes and woven baskets and other Balearic handicrafts. There's a great cafe-restaurant here, too (see 13 Map p70, C4). (www.canmiquelguasch.com; Ctra Ibiza Town–Sant Joan Km 9.2; 8.30am-1am)

Explore

Sant Antoni de Portmany & Around

Sant Antoni, widely known as 'San An', is about as Spanish as bangers and mash. While it's still known for booze-ups, brawls and lairy Brits abroad, it does have a more mellow side, particularly along the cafe-lined Sunset Strip, home of the legendary Café del Mar.

The Region in a Day

☀ Begin the day with a stroll along Sant Antoni's **promenade** (p90) before taking breakfast in stylish **Club Nàutic** (p91) overlooking the marina. There aren't many sights but do check out the **Església de Sant Antoni** (p89) and consider a session at **Surf House Ibiza** (p89).

☀ Next up it's a spot of beach-hopping. A car is ideal for exploring, but boats also run from the harbourfront to all the following beaches. West of town, gorgeous **Cala Conta** (p85), with its pellucid water, is a good choice, or try **Cala Bassa** (p85) for a more family-friendly cove. North of San An there's pretty **Cala Salada** (p85), while tiny Cala Gracioneta is a jewel, and home to the outstanding **El Chiringuito** (p92) for meals and drinks.

🌙 Celebrate the sunset at **Café del Mar** (p87) or **Kasbah** (p87) before enjoying authentic Ibizan food at **Es Rebost de Can Prats** (p91). After midnight check out what's on at either **Ibiza Rocks House at Pike's Hotel** (p92) or **Es Paradis** (p93).

◉ Top Experiences

Sant Antoni's Coastal Surrounds (p84)

Bar-Hopping in San An (p86)

🖤 Best of Sant Antoni de Portmany & Around

Bars

Ibiza Rocks House at Pike's Hotel (p92)

Café del Mar (p87)

Sunsets

Sunset Strip (p94)

Cala Conta (p85)

Kumharas (p93)

Cala Salada (p85)

Getting There

🚌 **Bus** L3 from Ibiza Town (every 15–30 min Jun–Oct, every 30–60 min Nov–Apr).

🚌 **Bus** L9 from airport (every 60 min Jun–Oct).

Top Experiences
Sant Antoni's Coastal Surrounds

There are wonderful sandy beaches close to Sant Antoni. The town boasts a sublime natural harbour ('de Portmany' means great port) and a reasonable beach, but there are better options for a day by the sea. Heading west, Cala Bassa is a gorgeous cove with sheltered turquoise water, though it can get busy. Calas Conta and Comte are further away, and enjoy some of the clearest, cleanest seas in Ibiza. To the north, Cala Salada is another gem of a beach.

Getting There

🚌 **Bus** L4 to Calas Conta and Comte (eight to nine daily May–Oct).

🚌 **Bus** L7 to Cala Bassa (eight to nine daily May–Oct).

⚓ **Ferry** From the harbourfront (every 30–60 min May–Oct for Calas Conta, Comte and Bassa).

Cala Bassa beach

Don't Miss

Cala Conta

Occupying a low-lying headland, the sublime beach of **Cala Conta** (Map p88, A3) has very shallow offshore waters which are fabulously clear and menthol fresh. The bay faces directly west, so it's a very popular place late in the afternoon when hundreds gather to watch the sun sink into the ocean, either from the coastal cliffs or at the bar-restaurant Sunset Ashram (p93).

Cala Comte

Just south of Cala Conta is a small cove known as **Cala Comte** (Map p88, A3), where there are two tiny beaches, one favoured by nudists; you'll find a *chiringuito* for snacks. Offshore is Illa des Bosc, 'Island of Woods', though its pines were cut down over a century ago. Strong swimmers can reach this island (it's around 400m away), but take care with sea currents and watch out for boat traffic.

Cala Bassa

Heading west and south from Sant Antoni, you'll come to the bay of **Cala Bassa** (Map p88, B3), a pretty swoop of sand backed by junipers and pines. It's popular for its turquoise water and blissed-out beach club. Walk in beyond the rocks to this lovely, sandy horseshoe bay.

Cala Salada

It's just 5km north of Sant Antoni, but the lovely cove of **Cala Salada** (Map p88, D1) feels a continent away. The coastal environment is spectacular here, with cliffs and soaring pine-clad hills sheltering the small sandy beach and a shoreside seafood restaurant. Clamber over the row of fisher's huts and you'll reach a second, even more peaceful cove: Cala Saldeta.

☑ Top Tips

▶ There's no public transport to any of these beaches between November and April.

▶ The route to Calas Conta, Comte and Bassa is flat and good for cycling.

✕ Take a Break

At Cala Conta, Sunset Ashram (p93) has a wonderful sea-facing terrace for a drink and there's also a simple snack bar at Cala Comte. Cala Salada's beach restaurant is fine, but you'll dine better at lovely El Chiringuito (p92) on Cala Gracioneta, 3km to the south.

Top Experiences
Bar-Hopping in San An

San An has enough bars – club-bars, lounges, pubs and even local bars – to drown the devil himself. There are three distinct areas: the 'West End' is a Brit-only territory of pubs and footy-shirt-clad drinkers that might as well have the Union Jack flying overhead. The renowned Sunset Strip has a more mellow vibe, while along the beach promenade there are lounge-style places.

1 Boho Haven

Beginning on San An's promenade, **Tulp** (Avinguda Dr Fleming; ⏱ 11am-2am May-Sep; 📶) is a cool beach bar with a zany colour scheme, shisha pipes and hammocks, plus Chesterfield sofas scattered with cushions for quality lounging. Don't expect a flower-power soundtrack – DJs spin purely electronic vibes. They serve reasonably priced grub; the set menu is just €12.95.

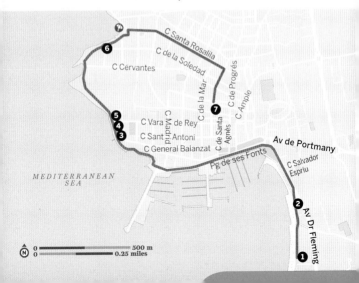

❷ Beachside Beats

Enjoying a prime beachfront location, **Ibiza Rocks Bar** (www.ibizarocks.com; Avinguda Dr Fleming; meals €10-18; ⏱11am-4am May-Sep) is a haven for music lovers with acoustic performances from the likes of Pete Doherty, and DJ sets from artists including Annie Mac and Basement Jaxx – in short, there's always a party fever brewing. During the day it's a cool spot for drinks and meals (including hearty breakfasts).

❸ Red-Hot Sunsets

It's a 10-minute walk from the north of the promenade, past the marina, to the Sunset Strip. With its horizon-facing vistas, glam decor and terrace, **Savannah** (www.savannahibiza.com; Carrer General Balanzat; ⏱11am-3am May-Oct; 📶) is a fine pick for a cocktail or a dining table with a sunset view. The intimate back room is a red-hot party venue (it's free to get in) and has hosted DJ talent including Roger Sanchez.

❹ The One and Only

The island's most famous bar, **Café del Mar** (www.cafedelmarmusic.com; Carrer Vara de Rey 27; ⏱4pm-midnight May–mid-Oct) is an Ibiza institution and a place of pilgrimage for many. The bar has been serving up the same mix of atmospheric electronic tunes, pricey drinks and staggering sunset views since 1980, growing to include a swanky adjacent bar-restaurant and a merchandise shop that (of course) sells the brand's world-renowned mixed CDs and assorted clobber.

❺ Mambo Mambo

Established in 1994 **Café Mambo** (www.cafemamboibiza.com; Carrer Vara de Rey 3; ⏱1pm-2am) is a music-geared venue with lots of preclub action, and the warm-up bar of choice for many globally famous DJs. The premises include a stylish twin-deck restaurant terrace (book ahead, minimum spend €70). Drinks are very expensive (around €15 a cocktail); try their *cava* (sparkling wine) sangria.

❻ Mellow Vibes

Kasbah (📞971 96 08 93; www.kasbahibiza.com; Carrer de la Soledad 68; mains €12–20; ⏱11am-midnight May-Oct) an attractive, modish bar-restaurant just north of the main Sunset Strip beside a small cove beach. It's perfect as a less-frenetic location for a sundowner, with good house wines to quaff and mellow background tunes. There's a great tapas selection as well as fish, meat and salad mains.

❼ Real Ale

Heading inland from the Sunset Strip, if you are in the mood for a real ale and full-monty British breakfast, look no further than the **Ship** (Plaça de s'Era d'en Manyà; ⏱10am-3am Apr-Oct). This welcoming Welsh-owned pub is very popular with workers doing the Ibiza season, so it's a good place to find out what's on. Drink prices are moderate and there are DJs and bands some nights. Just steps southwest of the Ship you'll find the notorious West End.

Cala Salada ◎

MEDITERRANEAN SEA

🞩 13

🞩 12

Cala Gracioneta
11 🞩 ◎ 4
Cala Gració ◎ 3
Aquarium Cap Blanc ◎

Sant Antoni de Portmany

See Sant Antoni de Portmany Enlargement

Sant Antoni Promenade ◎ 5
Surf House Ibiza ◎ 2
🞩 6

🞩 14

Port des Torrent ❋

C731

PM803

N
0   1 miles
0   2 km

For reviews see
◎ Top Experiences   p84
◎ Experiences   p89
🞩 Eating   p90
🖢 Drinking   p92
❋ Entertainment   p95

Caló des Moro 🞩 8
C Santa Rosalila
C Cervantes 19 ❋
Església de Sant Antoni
C Vara de Rey
C General Balanzat 🞩 7
🞩 10

C de Progrés
C Ample
f 9
◎ 1
f
18 ❋ Av de
Portmany
16 🖢 🖢 17
Pg de ses Fonts
Av Dr Fleming

Sant Antoni de Portmany

0   500 m
0   0.25 miles

Illa Sa Conillera

Illa des Bosc

Cala Conta ◎ 15
Cala Comte ◎
◎

Cala Bassa ◎

Cala Codolar ❋

Experiences

Església de Sant Antoni CHURCH

1 ⊙ Map p88, B2

There's been a church in this spot since 1305, but the existing structure is mainly from the 17th century. You approach the church via a lovely cobbled patio (check out the attractive adjoining porch). Its key features are its rectangular defence tower (cannons were once mounted here to deter pirates) and twin belfry. (Plaça de l'Església)

Surf House Ibiza SURFING

2 ⊙ Map p88, D3

There's very little surf in Ibiza but this bay-facing place has its own Flowrider wave machine so you can learn the ropes and get all Hawaii–Five-0. There are discounts for groups, sunbeds for chilling and they sell drinks and food too. (www.surfhouseibiza.com; Avinguda Dr Fleming; surfing per hr €30; ⊙noon-midnight; 🛜)

Aquarium Cap Blanc AQUARIUM

3 ⊙ Map p88, D2

This small, open-air aquarium has an assortment of local sea life including groupers and wrasse, octopuses and lobsters, moray eels and lots of starfish. Occasionally, injured turtles are allowed to recuperate here. There are boardwalks above the pools so you can get a close look. It's located in a former smugglers' cave around 1.5km north of the Sunset Strip. (www.aquariumcapblanc.com; Cala Gració; adult/child €4.80/2.80; ⊙10am-10pm May-Oct, 10am-2pm Sat Nov-Apr)

Understand

Conillera

The large, elongated island of Conillera can be seen from many points around Sant Antoni bay. It's uninhabited, but harbours a considerable population of rabbits (Illa Conillera means 'rabbit island' in Catalan), a unique species of wall lizard, and lots and lots of cicadas. Local folklore has it that this was the birthplace of Hannibal, the Carthaginian general, and there's a cave on its southern side that's nicknamed Can Anibal (Hannibal's House). Conillera is also said to be the best source of the narcotic plant *Hyoscyamus albus* (henbane) used by pagans for ceremonies during the night of Sant Joan. The island is only accessible by private boat.

In 2014 property developers proposed converting the island's only structure, a lighthouse dating from 1857, into a hotel. This scheme is being fought by environmentalists as the island is located in a marine reserve.

Cala Gració

BEACH

4 Map p88, D2

Within walking distance of Sant Antoni, this sheltered bay is fringed by pine woods and has a generously portioned stretch of white sand, shallow turquoise water and a bar-restaurant for snacks and drinks. It's about 1km north of **Caló des Moro**. On the north side of Gració, a path leads for 100m to a second gorgeous bay, **Cala Gracioneta**, which is even smaller, only 30m or so wide, but has fine, pale sand and a lovely restaurant: El Chiringuito (p92).

Sant Antoni promenade

AREA

5 Map p88, E3

San An's harbourside promenade has been extended in recent years and now stretches around the entire coastline from Caló des Moro in the north down past the Punta des Molí promontory (where there's an old windmill). One of the best sections borders s'Arenal beach, where there are bars, including Tulp (p86). (Avinguda Dr Fleming)

Eating

Casa Thai

THAI €

6 Map p88, E3

A down-to-earth, inexpensive Thai joint with authentic curries, stir-fries, noodle dishes and Singha beer at (almost!) Southeast Asian prices. There's a set menu for just €12. The premises are nothing fancy, with outdoor seating next

to a busy road. (☑ 971 34 40 38; Avinguda Dr Fleming 34; mains €7-11; ☺ 11am-11pm)

Rita's Cantina

INTERNATIONAL €

7 Map p88, A2

One of the most popular places in town, Rita's serves great breakfasts, Mexican food, Spanish favourites, baguettes (from €3.25), a terrific club sandwich and has lots of juice and smoothie choices. The front terrace is the place to be on a sunny day, facing the harbour. (www.ritascantina.com; Carrer Madrid 1; snacks/meals from €3/7.50; ☺ 8am-1am; 🛜)

Villa Manchego

SPANISH €

8 Map p88, A1

This is where you go when you want to escape the Brits Abroad crowds, a very local place with a straightforward

Sunset Strip (p94)

menu that includes tapas, meat and fish mains (try a fisherman's platter; €31 for two people), rice dishes and kids' plates. It's about a 15-minute walk north of the harbourfront. (www. villamanchega.com; Carrer Isidor Macabich 19; mains €9-16; ⏲noon-midnight)

Es Rebost de Can Prats IBIZAN €€

 9 Map p88, B1

Authentic, family-run Ibizan restaurants are a rare breed in Sant Antoni – all the more reason to visit Es Rebost. Go for spot-on mains like *arrós melós amb peix de roca* (creamy seafood rice with local rock fish), *parrillada de pescado* (mixed barbecued fish)

or a hearty *sofrit pagès* (country fry-up). The three-course day menu is a bargain at €15. Probably the best restaurant on the island for Ibiza cuisine. (📞971 34 62 52; www.esrebostdecanprats. com; Carrer Cervantes 4; mains €15-24; ⏲1-4pm & 8pm-midnight Wed-Mon)

Club Nàutic SPANISH €€

10 Map p88, B2

A respite from Sant Antoni's mean streets, this stunning modernist structure boasts the best view in town, with tables overlooking the marina and bay. The cafe section has a moderately priced menu, with good breakfasts, tapas and salads (from €11.60) while the polished glassware, starched tablecloths and gourmet menu in the restaurant next door draw the town's elite. (☎971 34 16 51; www.esnauticrestaurant.com; Passeig de la Mar; meals cafe/restaurant €12/30; ⏱8.30am-midnight; 🛜)

Villa Mercedes   FUSION €€

Set in gorgeous gardens, this boho-chic Ibizan mansion overlooks the marina and offers eclectic cooking, from wok-fried vegetables through rice and noodle dishes to the local catch of the day, as well as cocktails and live music most nights. (☎971 34 85 43; www.villamercedesibiza.com; Molls dels Pescadors; mains €15-26; ⏱1pm-2am)

El Chiringuito   MEDITERRANEAN €€€

11 🍴 Map p88, D2

In a hidden bay, with tables almost on the sand, this beautifully situated

---

Ⓠ Local Life
Can Pujol

At seafood restaurant **Can Pujol** (Map p88, C3; ☎971 34 14 07; www.restaurantecanpujolibiza.com; Carrer des Caló; meals €28-40; ⏱1-4pm & 7.30-11.30pm, closed Dec) the slightly run-of-the-mill appearance of the place belies the quality (and cost) of the cuisine, with lots of lobster dishes and fine *bullit de peix* (Catalan fish stew). No meat is served. The restaurant, which is 5km west of Sant Antoni near Port des Torrent, boasts great sunset views over the Mediterranean.

---

beach restaurant has a slightly casta-way, barefoot vibe (though its prices are more banker- than backpacker-friendly). It's perfect for seafood, with excellent paella (€52 for two) and great sangria. They hire out posh daybeds for luxe-lounging and play top tunes here. Located 2km north of central San An. (☎971 34 83 38; Cala Gracioneta; ⏱11am-11.30pm May-Oct; 🛜)

Sa Capella   SPANISH €€€

12 🍴 Map p88, E2

This upmarket, highly atmospheric and romantic restaurant occupies an 18th-century chapel and is equally popular with Ibiza's old money elite and the DJ set. Meat dishes like suckling pig, lamb chops, rib-eye steak and chateaubriand are beautifully cooked and presented and the wine list is amazing. (☎971 34 00 57; Ctra Sant Antoni–Santa Agnès Km 0.5; mains €18-38; ⏱8pm-midnight Apr-Oct)

Drinking

Ibiza Rocks House at Pike's Hotel   BAR

13 🍺 Map p88, E2

A legendary rural hotel that's hosted the likes of Freddie Mercury, Grace Jones and Bianca Jagger (and where Wham! filmed their Club Tropicana video), Pike's has been an A-list mecca for decades. In recent years the Ibiza Rocks team have injected a dose of 21st-century energy into the premises (a 15th-century farmhouse) and now

Pike's is once again one of Ibiza's coolest hang-outs.

The line-ups are superb, with Harvey resident DJ in 2015 and appearances from the likes of Greg Wilson and Crazy P as well as after-parties and gigs. And Pike's is simply a great place to party with huge open-air terraces for chilling, a cheeky karaoke room and intimate dance floor. (www.ibizarockshouse.com; Camí de Sa Vorera; ⏰ May-Oct; 🛜)

Kumharas

BAR

 14 Map p88, D3

On the far western side of Sant Antoni bay, around 5km from the centre, you can eat, drink and soak up the final rays at boho-cool Kumharas, with its hippy market, ethnic beats, Asian-style food and shisha pipes. It's something of an oasis in the heart of package hotel land, with DJs and live music (reggae, flamenco, world) most nights. (www.kumharas.org; Carrer de Lugo 2; ⏰ noon-2am May-Sep; 🛜)

Sunset Ashram

BAR

15 Map p88, A3

This mellow bar-restaurant enjoys a prime position for sunset. There's a DJ every night in season, with artists including Jon Sa Trinxa and Lenny Ibizarre spinning their magic. The food is OK, but the kitchen often struggles to cope in summer. It's great for a drink though; order a jug of sangria or a cocktail and you're set. (www.sunsetashram.com; Cala Conta; ⏰ 10am-midnight May-Oct)

 Top Tip

West End

Sant Antoni's prime (some would say primeval) bar enclave is the West End, a cluster of streets around Carrer Santa Agnès in the town centre. It's home to dozens of bars and pubs, many British-owned and virtually all of them British-geared. Don't expect to bump into many locals here. Drink prices are inexpensive, but the drunkenness, teenage antics and lairy behaviour certainly won't appeal to all.

Es Paradis

CLUB

 16 Map p88, B2

Go for the amazing sound system, fountains and outdoor feel. It's one of the prettiest of the macro-clubs, with loads of marble, greenery and a glass pyramid roof which defines the San An skyline. Es Paradis is known for its water parties (Tuesdays and Fridays); prepare to get soaked! (www.esparadis.com; Carrer Salvador Espriu 2; admission €15-50; ⏰ 11pm-6am)

Eden

CLUB

17 Map p88, B2

Despite its domes and minarets this is very much a temple of dance. Eden draws huge crowds of (British) clubbers for its big trance and techno nights: DJ Judge Jules has had a residency here for years. Inside there's a state-of-the-art sound system, a vast main dance floor and numerous podiums for the

Understand
Sunset Strip

Sant Antoni's Sunset Strip of chill-out bars is the most relaxed side of Ibiza's most notorious resort. For years this rocky coastline was the forgotten, back-end of town, but today it boasts a series of elegant bar terraces, and a smart promenade connects the various sections (which stretch for a kilometre or so between Carrer General Balanzat and the little bay of Caló des Moro to the north).

Until 1993 there was only one bar, the Café del Mar (p87), where pioneer resident DJ José Padilla spun vinyl and sold mix tapes to a small, well-informed bunch of music lovers, many from the UK. Essex-based DJ Phil Mison later took the helm and continued the mellow vibe. Café Mambo (p87) opened in 1994 and by the year 2000 there was a scattering of similar bars along the coast.

Café del Mar and Café Mambo remain the two best-known venues and attract the big crowds – thousands gather here in high season when BBC's Radio One bounces live DJ events back to the UK, television crews broadcast live shows and web cams beam the scene around the world. The commercialism is pretty relentless, with many bars now selling branded merchandise (Café del Mar even has its own emporium).

The sunset hype has exploded in the last decade or so and you'll now need to book a table for dinner (with a minimum spend) to reserve a space at the main bars. Or just bring your own drinks, find a patch on the rocks and tune in to your DJ of choice; many people choose to do this rather than paying the bars' inflated drinks prices. The sunset will remain the same, and when that giant ball of fire starts to dip into the Med to an accompaniment of electronic sounds, the spectacle and setting is still quite something.

Don't bother bringing your swimmers though; you'll have to scramble over sharp rocks for a dip along most of this coastline. The one spot where access is easy is the bay of Caló des Moro.

Understand
Electronic Mecca

San An has long been the 'entry level' point for young Brits in Ibiza. As the rest of the island goes increasingly upmarket, the town remains as down-to-earth as ever. In terms of ambience, San An retains an undeniable edge and energy; it's a destination where underground music finds a home, and where wannabe DJs will be given the opportunity to deliver in backstreet bars.

Backtrack to 1987, and all the main players who initiated the Acid House scene were holidaying in San An. Four soul boys from London – Danny Rampling, Paul Oakenfold, Nicky Holloway and Johnny Walker – found inspiration at Project and Milk bars in the town, discovered ecstasy, and raved to Alfredo's Balearic beats, under the stars, up the road in Amnesia (p47).

José Padilla and his eclectic, emotionally provocative DJ sets at the Café del Mar in the '80s and '90s really put San An on the map. A unique chill-out scene developed around José's cinematic, largely electronic sets, inspiring musicians across the globe. The CD series sold millions. Check out *Café del Mar: Volumen Dos* for an essential selection from that era.

club's dancers to perform their stuff. (www.edenibiza.com; Carrer Salvador Espriu; admission €20-45; ⏰midnight-6am May-Sep)

Plastik   BAR

 18 Map p88, B2

Right by the Egg roundabout, Plastik is one of the best club-bars in town, with quality DJs, an intimate dance floor and lots of pre-parties for the big clubs. It's unpretentious and draws a loyal British crowd. (www.plastikibiza.com; Avinguda Dr Fleming 5; ⏰11am-4am May–mid-Oct)

Entertainment

Ibiza Rocks Hotel   LIVE MUSIC

19 ⭐ Map p88, A1

Ibiza does indeed rock at this venue, with the best gigs on the island (Dizzee Rascal, The Prodigy and Arctic Monkeys have all starred in recent years). It's in a slightly bizarre location: bands perform in the central courtyard of a hotel. The full line-up is posted on the website. (www.ibizarocks.com; Carrer Cervantes 27; ⏰May-Oct)

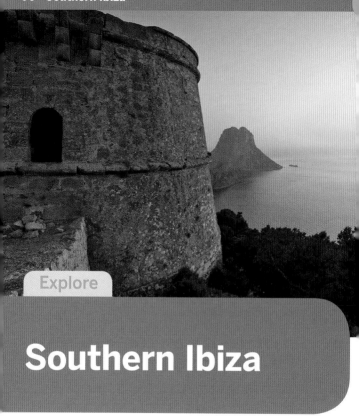

Explore

Southern Ibiza

Southern Ibiza has it all. This spectacular region includes the island's highest peak, its best sandy beaches and the enigmatic islet of Es Vedrà. It's a land of legends, ancient and modern, with a contemporary art installation called Stonehenge and the mystical sight of Atlantis. Factor in world-renowned clubs, bombastic beach bars and some amazing restaurants, and the South's appeal is unique.

The Region in a Day

☼ Enjoy breakfast in **Racó Verd** (p109) in pretty Sant Josep de sa Talaia before setting off to explore the stunning coastal region around **Es Vedrà** (p99). Climb up to the **Torre des Savinar** (p99) for an unparalleled view of the islet, catch a glimpse of **Atlantis** (p100) below, and check out the **Cova des Mirador** (p100) cave.

☼ Drive along Ibiza's stunning southern coastline, perhaps pausing at a cove or two on the way, such as **Cala Jondal** (p108). Then it's some beach time at glorious **Platja de ses Salines** (p103), where **Sa Trinxa** (p110) has a mellow vibe, and decent food and drinks. In the late afternoon stroll down to the **Torre de ses Portes** (p103). Later gawk at the **Salines** (p103); they are glorious around sunset.

☾ In the evening dine overlooking the waves at **Beach House** (p111) in Platja d'en Bossa, or at **Destino** (p109) in Sant Josep for a more modest setting (and bill). Then it's a drink at **KM5** (p111) before clubbing until dawn at **Space** (p111), **DC 10** (p111) or **Ushuaïa** (p111).

For a local's day exploring southern coves and villages, see p104.

◉ Top Experiences

Es Vedrà & Around (p98)

Salines Beach & Salt Flats (p102)

◯ Local Life

Road-Tripping Southern Coves & Villages (p104)

🖤 Best of Southern Ibiza

Beaches

Platja de ses Salines (p103)

Es Cavallet (p107)

Platja d'en Bossa (p107)

Cala d'Hort (p99)

Cala Vedella (p107)

Cala Llentrisca (p107)

Clubs

Space (p111)

DC 10 (p111)

Getting There

🚌 **Bus** L8 runs between Ibiza Town and Sant Antoni via Sant Josep (every 60 min, all year).

🚌 **Bus** Services connect Ibiza Town with a number of beaches including Platja d'en Bossa, Platja de ses Salines and Cala Vedella; check schedules at www.ibiza bus.com.

Top Experiences
Es Vedrà & Around

The scenery around Ibiza's southwestern tip is simply breathtaking. Offshore, the spectacular islet of Es Vedrà rises like a volcano from the azure Mediterranean, while its sister island, Vedranell, resembles a sleeping dragon. Opposite Vedrà is the lovely cove beach of Cala d'Hort. And just to the east are the evocatively situated defence tower Torre des Savinar and the simply extraordinary old quarry known as Atlantis.

👁 Map p106, A3

Getting There

🚌 **Bus** There's no bus service to the area.

🚗 **Car** Take an easy day trip exploring the area with a number of short, scenic drives and walks.

Cala d'Hort

Don't Miss

Rock Star

The stunning, vertiginous island of **Es Vedrà** (Map p106, A3) is one of the most startling sights in the Balearics, emerging abruptly from the Mediterranean. A real rock star, it's associated with numerous local myths and legends. The coastal road is surrounded by high mountains, so when Es Vedrà unexpectedly emerges into view, the effect is quite spellbinding.

Torre des Savinar

High above Vedrà, the **Torre des Savinar** (Map p106, A3) defence tower was constructed in 1763 to safeguard Ibiza's southern flank from pirate attack: it's also known (and signposted) as Torre d'en Pirata. The tower is a 10-minute walk uphill from the Cova des Mirador and boasts sweeping views directly over Vedrà and Vedranell, north to the island of Conillera, and southeast to pancake-flat Formentera.

Cala d'Hort

Nestled beneath the steep wooded hills of Ibiza's isolated southwestern corner, opposite Es Vedrà, the cove of **Cala d'Hort** (Map p106, A3) enjoys a privileged, isolated location. The beach itself consists of a strip of sand and pebbles, with quieter areas to the north and south. There are three good shoreside restaurants, including Es Boldado (p109).

Cala d'Hort beach sits within a national park, which was only established after a protracted campaign. Developers wanted to build a golf course and 420-bed hotel complex in this beautiful region, a plan that prompted huge demonstrations on the island (12,000 people, one in seven of the population, marched against it). After a

☑ Top Tips

▶ The Vedrà viewpoint, the caves, Torre des Savinar and Atlantis are only accessible on foot. Take the Torre des Savinar turn-off south of Cala d'Hort and park after 500m.

▶ Atlantis and both caves are revered by the spiritually minded, and should be treated with respect.

▶ To get to Es Boldado, there's a signposted side road just northwest of Cala d'Hort. Alternatively, it's a five-minute walk along the beach, past some fisher's huts.

✗ Take a Break

El Carmen (p109) specialises in fresh fish and rice dishes; it's just behind Cala d'Hort beach. Es Boldado (p109) offers more of the same with better views.

Understand

Es Vedrà

The subject of numerous myths and legends, the island of Es Vedrà is perhaps Ibiza's most enigmatic attraction. It's supposed to be highly magnetic (sailors have reported malfunctioning compasses as they near the island), and there have supposedly been numerous UFO sightings in the area. A pilot even diverted his flight in 1979, making an emergency landing in Valencia, after reporting strange lights and an unidentified object around Vedrà.

The island was linked with the Carthaginian love and fertility goddess, Tanit. Another legend has it that Vedrà could be the island of the sirens, the sea-nymphs who tried to lure Odysseus from his ship in Homer's epic. And a Carmelite priest, Father Palau i Quer, reported seeing visions of the Virgin Mary and satanic rituals here in the 19th century.

Vedrà has also graced the covers of several albums, including Mike Oldfield's *Voyager*. Oldfield lived in a villa in the hills behind Vedrà for years and later sold his house to Noel Gallagher.

12-year struggle the Cala d'Hort National Park was created in 2002 and the bulldozers were stopped.

Lost Civilisation?

A tiny rocky peninsula that's been nicknamed **Atlantis** (Map p106, A3) for decades, this remarkable place is actually a former quarry, but it's easy to see how beatniks and hippies viewed the oblique cut-stone outlines as the remains of a lost civilisation. Artistically minded visitors have added Hindu-style carvings to the rocks, and cliff jumpers plunge into the deep, cobalt water.

Caves

There are two caves opposite Vedrà. **Cova des Mirador** (Map p106, A3) is a tiny cavern directly below the main Vedrà viewpoint; many people leave offerings here and there are cushions where you can relax and gaze out over the island. **Cova de Buda** (Map p106, A3) is just above Atlantis, another place of sanctuary that's revered by the spiritually inclined. It's home to a remarkable Buddha image said to have been etched by a Japanese hermit.

Es Vedranell

Guarding its bigger sister Vedrà like a demon from a fantasy novel, the smaller island of **Es Vedranell** (Map p106, A3) is a jumble of jagged rocks. Its nickname, 'sleeping dragon', is fully justified and easy to understand – it's not hard to pick out its head and spiky backbone emerging from the water.

Es Vedrà

Top Experiences
Salines Beach & Salt Flats

The extreme southeastern tip of the island offers some stunning landscapes and two of Ibiza's very best sandy beaches. Most of this region is taken up with a dazzling expanse of salt pans, the island's major source of wealth for millennia. To the area's south are the back-to-back beaches of Platja de ses Salines and Es Cavallet, home to some great shoreside bar-restaurants, and an ancient defence tower. All of this region is now part of the Parque Natural de ses Salines.

◉ Map p106, E4

Getting There

🚌 **Bus** L11 connects Ibiza Town with Platja de ses Salines; eight to ten daily buses May–Oct, six buses weekly Nov–Apr. Check schedules at www.ibizabus.com.

Platja de ses Salines and salt pans

Don't Miss

Platja de ses Salines

Arguably Ibiza's best beach, **Platja de ses Salines** (Map p106, E4) is a fine strip of pale sand with glass-clear sea. It's backed by towering sand dunes and patches of sabina pine woodland. Here celebs, beach babes, Spanish footballers, party poseurs and all-comers work the bronzed, blissed-out look. The scene mutates slightly from north (which is more family friendly) to south (which has a more boho vibe and some nudism).

Salines Salt Pans

Just south of the airport, the shimmering pools of the **salines** (salt pans; Map p106, E4) were the island's main source of wealth until the tourism boom. As you approach Platja de ses Salines and Es Cavallet beaches you drive right across the main body of the salt flats, an unforgettable experience. Salt is still harvested here for export; you'll see it piled up close to the road.

Torre de ses Portes

From **Torre de ses Portes** (Map p106, E4), the 16th-century defence tower at Ibiza's southernmost tip, you can glimpse the islands that speckle the Es Freus strait separating Ibiza and Formentera. Among them are Illa des Penjats (Hangman's Island), where captured pirates were once sent to the gallows, and Illa des Porcs (Pig Island), where plump pigs smuggled over from Formentera were once kept.

☑ Top Tips

▸ There are large car parks (€4 to €5 all day per car) at both Es Cavallet and Platja de ses Salines. Both fill up quickly between mid-June and early September.

▸ It's around a 20-minute walk from the southern ends of both Es Cavallet and Platja de ses Salines to the Torre de ses Portes. There's no shade and nowhere for refreshments on the way.

▸ Drinks and meals are expensive at all the beachside *chiringuitos*. Consider bringing a picnic.

✗ Take a Break

On Salines beach Sa Trinxa (p110) is one of the island's best places to chill, with DJs every day. Over on Es Cavallet, La Escollera (p110) is a stylish bar-restaurant with a lovely aspect over the Mediterranean.

Local Life
Road-Tripping Southern Coves & Villages

This drive takes in some hidden coves, a pretty village, an archaeological site, modern sculpture and some outstanding coastal scenery. If you can time your arrival at Stonehenge for sunset, so much the better.

1 Sant Francesc de s'Estany

Start the trip in the little village of Sant Francesc de s'Estany, 6km south of Ibiza Town and close to the airport. This tiny settlement was a base for the workers of the surrounding *salines* (salt pans). You can gaze over the *salines,* which stretch for several kilometres to the east, and learn about the history of the salt trade and local environment in the **Centro de Interpretación** (Sant Francesc de s'Estany; admission

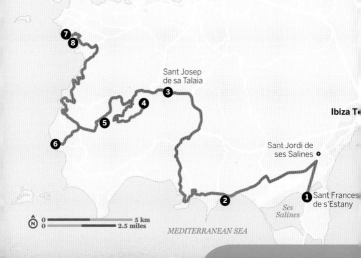

Sant Josep de sa Talaia

Ibiza T

Sant Jordi de ses Salines

Sant Frances de s'Estany

Ses Salines

MEDITERRANEAN SEA

0   5 km
0   2.5 miles

free; ◷10am-2pm & 6-9pm Tue-Wed & Fri-Sun Jun-Sep, 10am-2pm Sat & Sun Oct-May) here.

② Sa Caleta

This spot marks the first human settlement in Ibiza. In the mid-7th century BC, Carthaginians established a foothold at the **Sa Caleta archaeological site** (admission free), constructing a small hamlet by the sea. Beyond the metal railings are the foundations of buildings. Information panels explain the site's significance.

③ Sant Josep de sa Talaia

The prosperous village of Sant Josep has a pretty high street, several good cafes, restaurants and boutiques, and a relaxed ambience. While you're here check out the village church, the **Església de Sant Josep**, dating from 1726 – it boasts a three-storey facade with an impressive front porch.

④ Sa Talaiassa

Ibiza's highest peak, **Sa Talaiassa** (475m), is just southwest of Sant Josep. You can drive to the summit (the route is signposted from the Sant Josep–Cala Vedella road) for amazing vistas over the island, including the *salines,* and the Med, though you have to peer between gaps in the thick pine forest.

⑤ Roques Altes

Heading southwest from Sant Josep and Sa Talaiassa, the road descends through a delightful valley filled with orchards and olive groves then skirts the craggy, thickly wooded Roques Altes hills. Look out for exotic-looking hoopoe birds, which are common in this region.

⑥ Cala Carbó

There's not much to Cala Carbó, a mini-niche in Ibiza's southwestern coastline, its shoreline a mix of sand and pebbles. 'Carbó' means coal in Catalan: this bay was once used as a port for the import of coal from the mainland. You'll find good snorkelling offshore and a couple of seafood restaurants here.

⑦ Cala Codolar

The tiny cove of Cala Codolar, at the end of a (signposted) dirt track, boasts a sheltered sandy beach, with the headland to the north usually preventing the water from getting too choppy. There's a *chiringuito* for snacks and drinks. Cala Codolar is the jumping-off point for the Stonehenge monument, just a 10-minute walk to the south.

⑧ Stonehenge

Ibiza's most contemporary attraction is a stunning monument that locals have dubbed **Stonehenge** (Cala Codolar). This semicircle of 13 basalt columns were created by Australian artist Andrew Rogers and commissioned by Cirque du Soleil founder Guy Laliberté. One of the columns is 20m high with a gilded top. It's a perfect sunset spot, away from the crowds. Approaching the site you pass through a pair of ancient wooden doors, one inlaid with inscriptions in Arabic, which frame the island of Es Vedrà perfectly.

Sant Rafel

Ibiza Town

Figueretes

For reviews see

◆ Top Experiences — p98
◎ Experiences — p107
⊗ Eating — p109
🍷 Drinking — p110
🛍 Shopping — p113

Sant Josep
de sa Talaia

Sant Agustí
de Vedrà

⊗ 13

⊗ 10

Sa Talaiassa
(475m)

Sant Jordi de
ses Salines

Església de ⊙
Sant Jordi

24 ⓘ

22 4 Platja d'en
ⓘ ⊙ Bossa
⊙ 19 ⓘ 23
ⓘ 20

ⓘ 17

Sant Francesc
de s'Estany

18
ⓘ

✈ Airport

Ses
Salines

Salines 15 ⊗

Salt Pans

Platja de ⊙ ⊙ Es Cavallet
ses Salines ⊗ 1 ⊙ Es Cavallet
⊗ 16

Punta de

Cala
Codolar

Cala Tarida ⊙ 8

Cala Moll ⊙ 7

Cala ⊙ 2
Vedella

Cala
Carbó ⊙ 11
⊗ 12
Cala d'Hort

Cova des
Mirador Torre des Savinar
Cova de
Buda

Es Vedrà ⊙

Es Vedranell

Cap
Llentrisca

Cala
Llentrisca ⊙ 3

Cala
Lientrisca

Es Cubells

⊗ 14

Cala ⊙ 5
Cala
Jondal

Sa Caleta ⊙ 9
Sa Caleta Beach

ⓘ
21

MEDITERRANEAN SEA

5 km
2.5 miles

N

0
0

Experiences

Es Cavallet BEACH

1 Map p106, E4

On the eastern side of a narrow peninsula, the wonderful sandy beach of Es Cavallet is one of the island's finest. It was designated Ibiza's first naturist beach in 1978 and today it's the island's main gay beach. The northern section around La Escollera restaurant is more family geared, but the southern half is almost exclusively gay.

Cala Vedella BEACH

2 ◉ Map p106, A2

One of the most sheltered and attractive bays in Ibiza, gorgeous Cala Vedella lies at the rear of a deep inlet. It's a perfect spot for families, with a fine white sand beach, shallow water and a pedalo or two for fun. It's an upmarket resort, with low-rise hotels and villas dotted around the hills that fringe the bay and yachts gracing the turquoise sea. Buses run here from Sant Antoni, Ibiza Town and Sant Josep betweeen May and September.

Cala Llentrisca BEACH

3 ◉ Map p106, B3

The sublime horseshoe-shaped little bay of Cala Llentrisca is not accessible by road, but it's only a 10-minute walk from the nearest parking spot, southwest of Cala des Cubells. Occasionally,

Local Life
Es Torrent

One of Ibiza's secret coves, Es Torrent is 7km south of Sant Josep on the west side of the Porroig promontory. The beach's name comes from its position at the end of a *torrent* (seasonal river bed). Offshore from the sandy beach, the sea is shallow and a striking shade of blue. There's good snorkelling around the cliffs that fringe the bay. You'll find the upmarket Es Torrent (p110) seafood restaurant here, too.

a fisherman might turn up to use one of the huts by the shore, but most of the time you can expect real tranquility at this exquisite spot, backed by high wooded hills, with just the sound of the sea lapping the pebble shoreline breaking the silence.

Platja d'en Bossa BEACH

4 ◉ Map p106, E3

For decades Platja d'en Bossa was a pretty conventional bucket-and-spade resort aimed at holidaying families, but recent developments by the land-owning Matutes family have revolutionised the place, above all the opening of the glitzy club Ushuaïa. The beach, a 3km strip of pale sand, remains as lovely as ever. It is bookended by the Torre de Sal Rossa defence tower and the resort-suburb of Figueretes to the north.

Top Tip

DIY Mud Pack

Forget expensive spas – for a free beauty treatment fill a bucket with water and mix it with rich, muddy earth from the cliffs around bays such as **Xarraca**, Sa Caleta or Aigües Blanques (p65). The treatment is simple: cover yourself all over in the homemade mud pack, bake yourself in the Ibizan sun for 30 minutes until dry, and then dive into the sea to wash it all off.

Cala Jondal   BEACH

 5 Map p106, C3

Set between two lofty promontories, the exposed stony beach Cala Jondal doesn't look that attractive on first glance, but it was one of the first places to cash in on the booming beach club market and draws lots of celebs, yachties and the odd superstar DJ. Most of this rabble head to the Blue Marlin, an uber-posh beach club, but for a less glitzy, more affordable set-up Tropicana at the other end of the bay is a good choice.

Església de Sant Jordi   CHURCH

6 Map p106, E3

Located incongruously in the sprawling suburbs south of Ibiza Town, the fortress-like Església de Sant Jordi is well worth a quick diversion. There's been a chapel here since the 13th century, though the present structure – its colossal walls topped with full battlements to deter pirates – dates from the late 16th century.

Cala Molí   BEACH

7 Map p106, A2

Cala Molí is a sheltered cove beach with a sand-and-pebble shoreline and cobalt offshore waters. There's no bus service here so it rarely gets too busy (except in July and August). If you swim to the south side of the bay there's a small cave. The only structure here is a beach club with its own swimming pool and posh sun lounges.

Cala Tarida   BEACH

8 Map p106, A1

The beautiful bay of Cala Tarida boasts two beaches of golden sand and is surrounded by villas, family-friendly low-rise hotels and a swanky new beach club. It's a lovely scene, although, as there are good bus and boat connections to Sant Antoni it does get busy in the summer months.

Sa Caleta Beach   BEACH

9 Map p106, C3

Sa Caleta beach consists of three little bays: the main one has golden sand, loungers and umbrellas to rent while the other two tiny coves are pebbly and more secluded. At the back of the bay is Restaurante Sa Caleta, a low-key massage place and beachwear boutique. This beach is also known as Bol Nou.

Eating

Destino
TAPAS €

10 Map p106, C2

Offering perhaps the best tapas in Ibiza, this excellent, though small, place has lots of unusual, interesting dishes, very moderate prices and plenty of choice for vegetarians. Eat on the little terrace or in the atmospheric dining room. It's always very busy, so be sure to book ahead on summer nights. (971 80 03 41; Carrer Atalaya 15; meals €9-14; 7.30pm-midnight Mon-Sat;)

Es Boldado
SEAFOOD €€

11 Map p106, A3

Book a table for sunset and you'll enjoy one of Ibiza's most dramatic locations for a meal, with views over the island of Es Vedrà. Es Boldado is renowned for its seafood – you can't beat clams or steamed mussels to start – and grilled grouper fish, or opt for paella or *arroz a la marinera* (fishermen's rice). (626 494537; www.restauranteboldado.net; Cala d'Hort; mains €14-26; 1-4pm & 7.30-10.30pm)

Restaurante Sa Caleta
SEAFOOD €€

Steps from Sa Caleta beach (see 9 Map p106, C3), this excellent restaurant offers grilled and baked fish and lots of crustaceans and shellfish from the seawater tanks. Don't skip on the Ibizan desserts like *greixonera* and *flaó* and be sure to round off your meal in style with a Caleta coffee (p110). In the summer months there's often live music in the evenings. It's one of the few seaside restaurants that's open all year. (971 18 70 95; www.restaurantesacaleta.com; noon-midnight May-Oct, noon-7pm Nov-Apr)

El Carmen
SEAFOOD €€

12 Map p106, A3

With tables directly overlooking Es Vedrà and Cala d'Hort beach, El Carmen is highly popular for good reason. Offers lots of seafood and fresh fish, good rice dishes and tasty local bread and *alioli*. (971 18 74 49; Cala d'Hort; mains €13-26; 10am-2.30pm & 5-9pm Apr-Sep, shorter hours in winter)

Local Life

Racó Verd

Almost opposite Sant Josep's village church, **Racó Verd** (www.racoverdibiza.es; Plaça de l'Església; meals from €7; 10am-2am Mon-Sat mid-Mar–Oct, 10am-4pm Mon-Sat & evenings Fri & Sat Nov-Dec, closed Jan-Feb;) is the hub of the community. It hosts live music events (flamenco, jazz, Latin, bluesy rock) four nights a week at 9.30pm in summer. It's great for breakfast; try the *huevos rancheros* (spicy Mexican-style eggs), a ciabatta bread sandwich (€5 to €6) or a few tapas. There's a great terrace, with tables around an ancient olive tree.

Can Berri Vell

SPANISH €€

13 Map p106, C1

The setting, inside a 17th-century Ibizan *casament* (farmhouse), is highly atmospheric, with a warren of rooms and lots of historic features including metre-thick walls to admire. There's also a lovely terrace with views over Sant Agustí's village church. The cuisine is quite elaborate, with dishes like roasted turbot with caramelised carrots and white truffles. (971 34 43 21; www.canberrivell.es; Plaça Major; mains €14-24; 8pm-midnight Mon-Sat Apr-Oct, daily Jul-Aug)

Es Torrent

SEAFOOD €€€

14 Map p106, C3

Popular with a yachtie crowd, this fine seafood place sits at the back of a pretty cove. You'll be informed by the staff which fresh fish and seafood dishes are available. Specials include *la fideuà de pescado y marisco* (vermicelli-like noodles with fish and seafood). (971 80 21 60; www.estorrent.net; Es Torrent beach; mains €16-36; 1-10pm Apr-Oct)

La Escollera

SPANISH €€€

15 Map p106, E4

At the northern end of glorious Es Cavallet, this seafood restaurant has stunning views over white sands and across to Formentera from its terrace. Its paellas are great, and the John Dory with Ibizan-style potatoes is excellent. Live musicians and DJs add to the vibe. In high season service can be

Top Tip

Caleta Coffee

In restaurants across Ibiza, particularly in the south, you may come across Caleta coffee on the menu, a special *queimada* (Spanish punch). Making a memorable finish to a meal (unless you're driving), it's wonderfully aromatic and includes a generous dose of brandy, lemon and orange peel, and spices. Said to have been invented back in the 1950s by the owner of Restaurante Sa Caleta (p109), it should be prepared at your table, and is probably best sampled at its original location.

a struggle at times. (971 39 65 72; www.laescolleraibiza.com; Platja Es Cavallet; mains €15-30; 1-7pm, to midnight Jul-Aug;)

Drinking

Sa Trinxa

BAR

16 Map p106, E4

At the southern end of Salines beach, quite a walk from the parking lot, this is the island's coolest *chiringuito*. It draws quite a crowd – hardcore clubbers and fashionistas, the odd model and Ibizan hippie types – all soaking up the Balearic vibes of the resident DJs, who include Jon Sa Trinxa. Snacks and meals are served, too. (www.satrinxa.com; 11am-9pm May-Oct)

Beach House BAR

17 Map p106, E3

Is it a bar...beach club...restaurant? Way of life? Beach House is all of the above: one stylish unit that occupies a prime patch of shoreside real estate on the posh side of Bossa. The food is excellent (try the slow-roasted lamb), the crowd is cool, the DJs are world class (German label Diynamic were residents in 2015) and your bill will be expensive. (☎971 39 68 58; www.beachouseibiza.com; ⊙10am-1am May-Oct; 📶)

DC 10 CLUB

18 Map p106, E3

The rawest, least pretentious club in Ibiza, DC 10 is all about the music with a distinctly underground vibe. The door tax is relatively modest (for Ibiza!) and drinks are moderately priced compared to other big venues. Come for Circo Loco (Mondays), one of the best sessions in Ibiza, which kicks off early in the day. (Ctra Sant Jordi–Salines Km 1; admission €20-35; ⊙3pm-6am May-Oct)

Space CLUB

19 Map p106, E3

Space has won more awards than any other club in Ibiza and has been voted the Best Club in the World multiple times at the International Dance Awards. It was originally more of a day club, famous for its intimate open-air terrace, but today it's grown into a vast mecca of dance: 40 DJs are hired on some sessions and up to 8000 clubbers accommodated. Come for Carl Cox (Tuesdays). (www.space-ibiza.es; Platja d'en Bossa; admission €35-75; ⊙11pm-6am)

Ushuaïa CLUB

20 Map p106, E3

Queen of daytime clubbing, ice-cool Ushuaïa is a Vegas-style, open-air megaclub, with its vast VIP sections, conspicuous consumption and designer-clad hedonistas. Superstar DJs like David Guetta and Luciano get the party started early on. There's also poolside lounging with Bali beds, a Sky Lounge for sparkling sea views and a minimalist-cool hotel. (www.ushuaia beachhotel.com; Platja d'en Bossa 10; admission €40-75; ⊙3pm or 5pm-midnight; 📶)

KM5 BAR

21 Map p106, D3

This bar, named after its highway location, draws a very cool, fashionable

Top Tip

Keep Cool

Drinks are incredibly expensive (up to €10 for a small bottle of water) in Ibizan clubs and air-conditioning is insufficient, so the risk of overheating is a real concern. Budget for your night out accordingly, take on extra liquids and chill out when necessary (most clubs have outdoor terraces). You can't take your own water into clubs.

Understand

Ibiza's Salt Pans

First developed by the Phoenicians, Ibiza's spectacular **salt pans** were the island's only reliable source of income for over 2000 years. Romans and other invaders maintained the pools, but it was the Moors, experts at hydraulic technology, who developed the system of sluice gates, mills and channels.

Salt has been of vital importance since antiquity, essential for health and preserving food, and Southern Ibiza is perfect terrain for salt production. Seawater is pumped in during May, left to evaporate for three months and then harvested in August. The water level has to be perfect – if it evaporates too quickly there will be little salt residue. A rainy summer will also harm salt production – if the water is not saline enough it will not crystallise into salt. If conditions are right a crust of pink-white powder develops, which is stored in huge salt mounds, then exported.

Originally salt was traded from nearby Platja d'en Bossa, from a bay called Sal Rossa (Pink Salt). But in the late 19th century a new jetty was built at La Canal on the north side of Salines beach, and a steam engine was brought in to help shift the salt. Until that time everything had been done manually, with labourers toiling in the extreme August heat. Today tractors, trucks and conveyor belts perform the hard graft, and the salt pans employ a few dozen rather than hundreds of employees. Ibizan salt is a popular souvenir; you can purchase **Sal de Ibiza** (www.saldeibiza.com) from shops across the island.

Natural Reserve

The salt flats, which cover over 400 hectares, now form part of the the Unesco-listed Parque Natural de ses Salines, a nature reserve of marshes, salt pans and coast that encompasses Southern Ibiza and Formentera. The salt pans are an important wetland habitat for birds, and a refuelling stop for migrating storks, herons and flamingos. Two hundred bird species are found here year-round, including ospreys and black-necked grebes. The **Centro de Interpretación** (Sant Francesc de s'Estany; admission free; ☯10am-2pm & 6-9pm Tue-Wed & Fri-Sun Jun-Sep, 10am-2pm Sat & Sun Oct-May) in Sant Francesc is dedicated to the Salines environment and salt trade.

set who love to lounge in the beautiful garden terrace with its Bedouin-style tents. There's also a top-drawer Mediterranean restaurant here should you need a bite to eat (and have the funds) and some DJ dance floor action some nights. (www.km5-lounge.com; Carretera de Sant Josep Km 5.6; ⏰8pm-4am May-Sep; 🛜)

Sankey's
CLUB

22 📍 Map p106, E3

This unpretentious club in Platja d'en Bossa has taken off in recent years as its DJ line-up has improved and the resort has attracted more and more clubbers. We Love (for years a clubbing institution at Space) even shifted here in 2015. There are three rooms and a roof terrace. It draws a predominantly British crowd. (sankeys ibiza.info; Carrer de les Alzines 5; admission €30-40; ⏰midnight-6am May-Sep)

Bora Bora Beach Club
BAR

23 📍 Map p106, E3

Beachside bar where sun and fun worshippers work off hangovers and prepare new ones. Entry's free and the ambience is party fever with phat beats bouncing over the beach. It can get very messy here with thousands of swimwear-clad punters going for it under the Ibizan sun and jets (the airport runway is *very* close) screaming overhead. (www.boraboraibiza.net; Carrer d'es Fumarell 1; ⏰noon-6am May-Sep)

Local Life
Mercat d'Hippodrome

Ibiza is full of cheesy overpriced 'hippy' markets but the **Mercat d'Hippodrome** (⏰9am-3pm Sat) in Sant Jordi is a gloriously quirky affair. Held in the dust bowl of an old horse-and-buggy racetrack, it's full of stuff you probably don't really need, but is lots of fun to browse. Some of the secondhand clothes and books are neat. Buses between Ibiza Town and Platja de ses Salines pass by.

Shopping

Vino y Co
WINE

24 🔒 Map p106, E2

Wine specialist with often over 30 wines open for tasting, including many Ibizan bottles. There's a bar here too, so you can linger a while and enjoy a tapa or two. (vinoyco.com; Ctra Ibiza Town–Sant Josep Km 1.6; ⏰10am-2pm & 5-8pm Mon-Fri, 10am-2pm Sat; 🛜)

Explore

Formentera

Offering pure get-away-from-it-all escapism, the Formenteran pace of life is blissfully languid. Tourism here is strongly tied to environmental ethics, with hotel numbers restricted, construction controlled and most visitors getting around on two wheels. There's not much in the way of culture (and very little nightlife), so it's the perfect place to enjoy barefoot living and some of Europe's very best beaches.

The Region in a Day

Begin in the pretty island capital of Sant Francesc with a leisurely breakfast at **Ca Na Pepa** (p121), then check out its boutiques, including **Muy** (p123), and **Alma Gemela** (p125) for Formentera espadrilles.

It's beach time. You can't beat the ravishing stretches of sand on the idyllic Trucador Peninsula; take your pick from either **Platja Illetes** (p117) or **Platja Llevant** (p117) and marvel at their mirage-like crystalline waters. Consider wading over to **Espalmador** (p117) island (or catch a boat instead) to savour the lovely cove Platja de S'Alga and wallow in the mud bath.

Postbeach, head up to the La Mola peninsula to see its famous **lighthouse** (p119). Then it's a quick backtrack to **Platja de Migjorn** (p119) for a sunset drink at either **Blue Bar** (p123) or **Chiringuito Bartolo** (p123). In the evening head to Sant Ferran for local cuisine at informal **Can Forn** (p121), followed by a late-night drink at old hippy hang-out **Fonda Pepe** (p123), where there might be some live music.

 Top Experiences

Trucador Peninsula (p116)

♥ Best of Formentera

Getting There

⚓ **Ferry** From the mainland **Baleària** (www.balearia.com) operates a direct ferry connection, Dénia–Formentera (1–2 daily; 2hr 30min; May–Sep). Three companies operate ferries from Ibiza Town (every 20–30 min May–Oct, hourly Nov–Apr; 30 min). Day-trip boats (May–Sep) run from most Ibiza resorts, and from the towns of Sant Antoni and Santa Eulària.

✈ **Air** There's no airport on Formentera.

Top Experiences
Trucador Peninsula

With white sands and truly turquoise water, the astonishing beauty of the pencil-thin Trucador Peninsula has to be seen to be believed. Sublime Illetes beach occupies one side of this narrow sliver of land, while on the eastern coast – just a few steps away – is equally lovely Platja Llevant. In high season these back-to-back beach twins do get very busy, but, such is the beauty of the scene, they're still an essential experience.

⊙ Map p118, B1

Getting There

🚌 Bus L7 runs between La Mola and La Savina via Illetes. Check schedules at busformentera.com.

🚤 Boat Three daily boats connect La Savina with Illetes and Espalmador. There are also daily boat connections from most Ibizan resorts to both Illetes and Espalmador.

Platja Illetes

Don't Miss

Platja Illetes

Forming the western section of the peninsula the simply stunning **Platja Illetes** (Map p118, B1) is as close to a vision of the Caribbean (minus the coconut trees) as you could imagine in Europe. With its blinding white sand and translucent waters, you won't want to move on in a hurry. Just offshore are the two small *illetes* (islets), Pouet and Rodona, that give the beach its name. In high season expect lots of day trippers from Ibiza.

Platja Llevant

Over the steep sand dunes on the eastern side of the Trucador Peninsula, **Platja Llevant** (Map p118, B1) is a remarkable, undeveloped beach. The powdery sand is so white that it dazzles your eyes, and the water is incredibly clear. It's also very shallow, so it's safe for children, and the sea warms up to bathtub temperatures on summer days.

Es Pas

The northerly tip of Formentera, Es Pas (The Crossing), is a magical place where the beaches of Llevant and Illetes combine and form a (partially submerged) 300m sandbar that stretches across to the island of Espalmador. There's usually a number of people making their way over, holding their belongings on their heads, when the sea is calm.

Nearby: Espalmador

A low-slung island of dunes and sandstone, Espalmador has a beautiful crescent-shaped beach of fine white sand, Platja de S'Alga, that's lapped by shallow water. While you're here you could check out the mud pond just north of the beach, though in summer it can get pretty dry.

☑ Top Tips

▶ There's almost no natural shade on the entire peninsula. Umbrellas and loungers can be hired but are in limited supply; consider bringing your own.

▶ All the restaurants here are pricey and packed in summer; think about bringing your own supplies.

▶ If it's calm you can usually wade over to Espalmador (the sea is usually waist-high for adults), but conditions are not always favourable.

▶ The Trucador Peninsula is part of the **Parque Natural de ses Salines** (☏ 971 30 14 60; www.balearsnatura. com). The coastal environment is fragile; avoid the roped-off areas and use the boardwalks.

✕ Take a Break

An ancient windmill, known as the Es Molí de Sal (p122), which used to pump seawater into the nearby salt pans, is today a renowned seafood restaurant at the foot of Illetes. Over on Llevant there's Restaurante Tanga (p122).

Trucador Peninsula

Platja
Illetes

Platja
Llevant

18 16

Salines

7

Es Pujols

17 3

For reviews see
Top Experiences	p116
Experiences	p119
Eating	p121
Drinking	p123
Shopping	p123

5 km

2.5 miles

N

0

0

MEDITERRANEAN SEA

*Far de
sa Mola*

4
Punta
sa Ruda

Es Pilar
de la Mola

15

27

14

Sa Talaia
(192m)

22

Es Arenals

6 Es Caló de
Sant Agustí

21

20 1

Platja de Migjorn

Es Ca Marí

13

Sant Ferran de ses Roques

Formentera

19 12 9 Guitars

Cala Saona

5

Sant Francesc Xavier 10

Església de
Sant Xavier

Museu
Etnològic

23 11

24
25
26

8

La Savina

Cala
Savina

Estany
d'es Peix

Estany
Pudent

Experiences

Platja de Migjorn   BEACH

 1 Map p118, C3

The island's entire southern arc is fringed with sandy bays known collectively as Platja de Migjorn. Development (and clothes) are kept to a bare minimum on this swath of coast, beloved of naturists and escapists. Some of the best beaches are at the eastern end around Es Arenals. A series of sandy tracks lead to Migjorn from the main island highway. Buses run to Ca Marí and Club Maryland.

Cap de Barbària   AREA

2 Map p118, A4

The Balearic's southernmost point is an extraordinary lunar-like landscape of parched rocky terrain that ultimately ends in a lighthouse. Gazing out to sea (next stop Africa!) and watching the waves crash against the cliffs below is captivating, especially at sunset. From the far (lighthouse) it's a 10-minute walk eastwards to the Torre d'es Cap de Barbària, an 18th-century watchtower.

Es Pujols   VILLAGE

3 Map p118, B2

Once a sleepy fishing village, Es Pujols is now the closest Formentera comes to a proper beach resort; it's very popular with Italians and Germans. Rows of sun-bleached timber boat shelters line the beachfront and there's a little bar zone and club here. If the beaches are too crowded for your liking, more-secluded options lie within easy striking distance (keep walking northwest towards Platja de Llevant).

Far de sa Mola   LIGHTHOUSE

4 Map p118, E4

Positioned high over the Mediterranean, the Far de sa Mola lighthouse defines the eastern edge of the island. There's a monument to Jules Verne (who used the end-of-the-world setting in one of his novels), the great Codice Luna (p121) bar-restaurant and a sublime seascape.

Cala Saona   BEACH

5 Map p118, A3

Delectable Cala Saona is a lovely cove on the west side of the island where the water is a startling shade of luminous blue and the sand salt white. However, you'll have to put up with the looming presence of the concrete Hotel Cala Saona which dominates the back of

 Top Tip

Tourist Information

Formentera's main **tourist office** (☏971 32 20 57; Carrer de Calpe; ☺9am-7pm Mon-Fri, to 3pm Sat & Sun May-Oct, 10am-2pm & 5-7pm Mon-Fri Nov-Apr) is beside the ferry landing point in La Savina. There are smaller branches in Es Pujols and opposite the church in Sant Francesc Xavier.

the bay. The turn-off for Saona is sign-posted off the Cap de Barbària road.

Es Caló de Sant Agustí BEACH

6 Map p118, D3

The tiny fishing hamlet of Es Caló occupies a rocky cove ringed by faded timber boat shelters. It served as the port for communities in La Mola for centuries. The coastline is jagged, but immediately west you'll find stretches of blisteringly white sand massaged by translucent water; this beach is known as Ses Platgetes.

Understand
Alternative Formentera

Formentera has a strong counterculture heritage. During the Spanish Civil War, anti-Francoists were housed in a concentration camp here (the ruined remains, called Es Campament, are just east of the capital Sant Francesc on the island's main highway); many stayed on after the war. During the 1970s, South American opponents to military rule fled here. Bob Dylan, King Crimson (who recorded the track 'Formentera Lady') and Pink Floyd (their album *More* features a Formentera windmill on its cover) were regulars in the 1960s. The autobiographical *Dope in the Age of Innocence* by Damien Enright is an excellent account of the early hippy era in Formentera.

Salines LAKE

7 Map p118, B1

Formentera's salt pans haven't been used for salt production since 1984 but salt crystals still form in the pools naturally. They form an important wetland zone for bird life including waders and gulls, as well as the odd visiting flamingo (August to October is the best time to spot the latter).

Museu Etnològic MUSEUM

8 Map p118, B3

The Museu Etnològic is a modest ethnological museum illustrating Formentera's agricultural and fishing heritage. (☎971 32 26 70; Carrer de Jaume I 17; admission free; ⏰10am-2pm & 5-7pm Mon-Fri, 10am-2pm Sat)

Formentera Guitars COURSE

9 Map p118, C2

Based in the village of Sant Ferran, this workshop offers three-week courses which enable you to craft a bass or guitar by hand. (www.formentera-guitars.com)

Església de Sant Xavier CHURCH

10 Map p118, B2

On Sant Francesc's idyllic central square this fortress-church has a stark, whitewashed facade; cannons were mounted on its roof until 1860. (Plaça de sa Constitució)

Top Tip

Accommodation

Formentera looks like a beautiful spot to pitch a tent, but, alas, camping is prohibited, to help preserve the island's fragile coastline. With strictly limited numbers of *hostales* and hotels, beds are like gold dust in midsummer and are often booked out in a flash. Reserve ahead!

Rental apartments are a better deal for stays of a week or more. Check out www.formenterahotels guide.com and www.guiaformentera.com. **Astbury Formentera** (www.formentera.co.uk) is a UK-based specialist in house and apartment rentals in Formentera.

Eating

Codice Luna   CAFE €

By La Mola's lighthouse (see 4 ◎ Map p118, E4), Codice Luna is a beautifully designed cafe-restaurant, its lovely terrace offering horizon-filling views of the Mediterranean. A tapas-style menu (including lots of bruschetta) is offered between 12.30pm and 4.30pm. It hosts a party every full moon (in the summer season) with DJs (and often free paella). (www.codiceluna.com; snacks €5-10; ☺10am-11pm Apr-Oct)

Lucky   CAFE €

A classic Balearic *chiringuito* (beach bar) with inexpensive prices that does a roaring trade in high season.

The terrace is tiny, so be prepared to wait, but the food is simple and tasty, including salads (€8 to €10), burgers (from €7.50), tortilla and focaccia bread sandwiches. It's at the end of the same sandy track as the Blue Bar (see 20 ⊕ Map p118, C3). (Carretera Sant Ferran–La Mola Km 7.9; mains €7.50-15; ☺11am-9pm May-Oct)

Ca Na Pepa   CAFE €€

 11 ⊗ Map p118, B2

Right next to the town's fortress-cum-church this place has a delightful terrace shaded by brushwood with (carefully) mismatched seating. You could spend the entire day munching through the menu, which features croissants and fruit salads for breakfast, bagels and *bocadillos* (filled rolls) and wraps for lunch, and lots of good dinner options. There's an excellent selection of wine by the glass. (www. canapepa.com; Plaça de sa Constitució 5; snacks €2.50-8, meals €15-30; ☺8.30am-11pm; ☎)

Can Forn   FORMENTERAN €€

 12 ⊗ Map p118, C2

Family-run Can Forn rustles up authentic island cuisine and has a cosy, old-school vibe. Go for dishes such as *calamar a la bruta* ('dirty calamari'; with potato, Mallorcan sausage and squid ink), local lamb chops and *habas* (broad beans) fried up with onions and garlic. (☎971 32 81 55; Carrer Major 39; mains €10-15; ☺noon-2.30pm & 7-11pm Mon-Sat)

Sa Platgeta
SEAFOOD €€

13 Map p118, B3

Planted amid pines just back from a narrow, rock-studded beach, this simple bar-restaurant is one of the best spots on the island for fresh fish. It's 500m west of Es Ca Marí (follow the signs through the backstreets or take the waterfront boardwalk). (☑971 18 76 14; Es Ca Marí; mains €15, meals €35; ☺1pm-midnight May-Sep)

Restaurante El Mirador
SPANISH €€

14 Map p118, D4

Has a great terrace from where you can watch the sun sink over Formentera. There's lots of grilled meats and fresh fish on the menu. (elmiradordeformentera.com; Carretera La Mola Km 14.3; meals €15-28; ☺10am-1am)

Pequeña Isla
SPANISH €€

15 Map p118, E4

Pequeña Isla, the 'Little Island', has a shady roadside terrace and serves up hearty meat items, fresh grilled fish, paella and other rice dishes, as well as various island specialities, including simmered lamb and fried octopus. (☑971 32 70 68; www.laislapequena restaurant.com; Avinguda del Pilar 101, La Mola; meals €27-40; ☺11am-11pm Tue-Sun)

Restaurante Tanga
SEAFOOD €€

16 Map p118, B1

Steps from the shore on Platja Llevant, Tanga has great fish including

Local Life
S'Eufabi

S'Eufabi (Map p118, D3; ☑971 32 70 56; www.seufabi.com; Carretera La Mola Km 12.5; mains €10-18; ☺noon-3.30pm & 8-11pm) dishes up some of the best paella and *fideuá* (a fine noodle) on Formentera, at a reasonable price. This shady eatery is about 1km east of Es Caló de Sant Agustí, on the left as you begin the gentle ascent towards Es Pilar de la Mola.

grilled grouper and dorado and tasty grilled paella. The house salad (mixed greens with slivers of salmon and cod) is a fine starter and there are meat dishes (try the pork tenderloin with green pepper) for those who really don't want seafood. (www.restaurantetanga.com; mains €14-28; ☺9am-8pm May-Oct)

Bocasalina
MEDITERRANEAN €€

17 Map p118, B2

This glass-fronted waterfront restaurant rustles up homemade pasta, spot-on seafood and steaks. Snag a candlelit table on the terrace overlooking the sea. (☑971 32 91 13; Passeig Marítim; mains €13-33; ☺9am-1.30am mid-Apr–Sep)

Es Molí de Sal
SEAFOOD €€€

18 Map p118, B1

In a tastefully renovated mill, Es Molí de Sal boasts a lovely terrace and magnificent sea views. It serves some of Formentera's finest seafood, salads, plus a few meat and pasta choices.

Try one of the rice dishes (like *arroz negro*) or house speciality, *caldereta de llagosta* (lobster stew). Expensive, but worth a splurge. (☎971 18 74 91; www.esmolidesal.es; Platja Illetes; meals €35-55; ☺noon-10pm May-Oct)

Drinking

Fonda Pepe
BAR

19 Map p118, B2

An island classic and said to be a former Dylan hang-out, Fonda Pepe is a knockabout bar that attracts a lively crowd of locals and travellers. It does great *pomadas* (shots of gin and lemon), serves simple grub at moderate prices and its walls are covered in photos from the good ol' hippy days. (Carrer Major 55; ☺10am-1am)

Blue Bar
BAR

20 Map p118, C3

This funky, sea-splashed shack is prime sunset cocktail material. Back in the '60s, legend says it even played host to the Floyd and King Crimson. Everything is blue – seats, sunshades, tables, loos and walls. Why, they even mix a blue Curaçao-based cocktail! Take the sandy track at Km 7.9 of the Carretera Sant Ferran-La Mola. (☎666 758190; www.bluebarformentera.com; ☺noon-4am Apr-Oct; ☺)

Tipic
CLUB

Formentera only has one real club, located at Es Pujols (see 3 Map p118,

B2), but it's a good one, an intimate space which draws a surprisingly good roster of DJs: Sven Väth's Cocoon had a residency here in 2015. (www.clubtipic.com; Avinguda Miramar 164; admission €20-45; ☺11pm-6am May-Oct)

10.7
BAR

21 Map p118, C3

Milan meets the sea at this super-stylish Italian number, with a menu of sushi and international wines. The rolling waves below, black-and-white decor and good vibes are perfect for lingering. Take the dirt track at Km 10.7 of the Carretera San Ferran–La Mola, off the PM820. (☎660 985248; www.10punto7.com; ☺11am-1am late May-Sep; ☺)

Chiringuito Bartolo
BAR

22 Map p118, D4

Chiringuito Bartolo, at the eastern extremity of the beach, must be the world's tiniest beach bar, and is much loved by islanders. Sitting cheerfully on stilts, it hosts two longish tables. Bartolo serves up drinks and snacks to wander away with if there's nowhere to sit. (Platja de Migjorn; ☺10am-sunset May-Oct)

Shopping

Muy
CLOTHING

23 Map p118, B2

Exquisite store owned by Alessandro Negri, the island's most famous designer. All the earthy, barefoot-style

Understand

Island Life Orientation

Formentera has a population of just 11,000, and only three settlements that could realistically be called villages. The current number of inhabitants actually represents something of a boom, for as recently as 2005 there were only 7500. The island has always been a sparsely populated place – it was completely abandoned for 300 years between the late 13th century and 1697 due to pirates and plague outbreaks. Quite how it got its name, said to be derived from the Latin word *frumentarium* (granary), is a mystery as its climate is unrelentingly arid and its rainfall meagre.

The island's microcapital, **Sant Francesc Xavier** (Map p118, B2), is a beautiful little settlement, with local life concentrated around its idyllic central square. This is where you'll find the village's fortress-church, Església de Sant Xavier (p120), which has a stark, whitewashed facade; cannons were mounted on its roof until 1860. Close by, the Museu Etnològic (p120) illustrates Formentera's agricultural and fishing heritage.

Three kilometres to the east, sleepy **Sant Ferran de ses Roques** (Map p118, B2) has a charming church with an exposed stone facade, and a simple belfry which looks out over a humble little plaza. The village has a handful of low-key cafes and restaurants. Back in the swingin' 1960s, Sant Ferran was a stop on the hippy trail, and Pink Floyd are said to have had their guitars custom-made here – a workshop still exists; check out Formentera Guitars (p120). The purple haze has lifted somewhat, but Sant Ferran still retains some hippy hippy shake, particularly at the bohemian Fonda Pepe (p123).

Es Pilar de la Mola (Map p118, E4) is the only settlement in the La Mola peninsula, an elevated limestone plateau; most of its coastline is only accessible by boat. The village has a graceful whitewashed 18th-century church and a few places to eat. It comes alive for its twice-weekly art market (p125).

Hippy market at Es Pilar de la Mola

furnishings, organic cotton clothing, gorgeous shoes and sandals, jewellery and accessories (cork-framed sunglasses anyone?) are very, very tasteful indeed. Look out for the vintage motorbike outside. (🕿971 32 16 22; Carrer Sant Joan 55; ⏰10am-2pm & 6-9pm May-Oct)

Alma Gemela
SHOES

24 🔒 Map p118, B2

Alma Gemela' means soulmate in Spanish and this lovely little boutique lives up to its name, specialising in espadrilles, which come in a riot of colours and an amazing range of styles including *Payesa* (traditional, and made in Formentera). Also sells great bracelets and jewellery. (🕿946 11 26 60; Carrer d'Isidor Macabich 9; ⏰10am-2pm & 5-10pm May-Sep)

Full Moon
CLOTHING

25 🔒 Map p118, B2

Look out for the sky blue doors and whitewashed facade of this stylish shop, which sells fab sunglasses, strappy shoes, floppy straw hats, classic woven baskets and chic kaftans, bikinis and scarves. (🕿971 32 23 76; Carrer Eivissa 6; ⏰10am-2pm & 5-10pm Mon-Sat, 10am-2pm Sun May-Sep)

Freak
SHOES

26 🔒 Map p118, B2

Zany little boutique just off the main square which stocks a good range of Havaianas, sandals, bags, hats, beachwear and sunglasses. (Avinguda Port Saler ⏰10am-9pm May-Oct)

Art Market
MARKET

27 🔒 Map p118, E4

Es Pilar de la Mola comes alive for its twice-weekly art market, which features lots of good locally made crafts. There's usually some live music, too. (Es Pilar de la Mola; ⏰4-9pm Wed & Sun)

The Best of
Ibiza

Formentera (p114)
LUNAMARINA / GETTY IMAGES ©

Best Walks
Santa Eulària to Punta Arabí

🏃 The Walk

The sparkling coastline around Santa Eulària, eastern Ibiza, is rewarding to explore. Its indented shoreline is rich in cove beaches, cafe-restaurants and places of interest. This walk starts in the urban surrounds of the town itself and then gradually becomes more rural, passing quiet beaches and patches of woodland. On the whole it's easy to follow; you'll be right on the shore for most of the route, and only have to skirt around the odd building. There's a minor historic sight en route, but it's mostly about the coastline itself, with plenty of opportunities for a swim along the way.

Start Promenade Santa Eulària

Finish Club Punta Arabí

Length 5km; two hours

✕ Take a Break

The attractive bay of Cala Pada is a great place to refuel, with a choice of places to eat right on the beach. Or around a kilometre east of here there's a boho beach shack, **Chirincana** (www.chirincanaibiza.com; meals €12-18; 🕑9am-2am, food served noon-5pm, 8pm-midnight May-Oct) on Cala Martina.

❶ Promenade

Begin the walk where the town's small river, the **Riu de Santa Eulària**, meets the sea. Head east of here following the town's lovely **promenade**, planted with palm trees, and the two arcs of sand which comprise Santa Eulària's beach. You'll pass the excellent cafe **Passion** (p56) on the way, should you want an energy-boosting coffee or juice, or there are many other options.

❷ Punta de s'Església Vella

After about 15 minutes you'll pass the town's attractive marina, where there's a cluster of cafes and restaurants, and then approach the rocky promontory of **Punta de s'Església Vella**, which juts into the Mediterranean. Legend has it that a medieval chapel once stood here, and that the structure collapsed seconds after the congregation departed Mass.

❸ Cala Niu Blau

The walk loops around the land side of Sol Beach House Hotel, and soon reaches attractive **Cala Niu Blau** (Blue Nest Cove), where there's a 100m stretch of fine sand and the **Pura Vida Beach Club**, a swanky place that serves expensive fusion food. On the eastern edge of this beach is a tiny *torrent*, a seasonal river bed that's dry in summer.

④ Cala Pada

The next section is partly shaded by coastal pines, and passes a couple of small promontories and some fine villas before you reach popular **Cala Pada** (p56). This lovely beach has fine white sand, sun lounges (€4.50 per day), three cafe-restaurants, and boat links to Santa Eulària and Es Canar.

⑤ s'Argamassa

Beyond Cala Pada the coastal path heads through the small, upmarket enclave of **s'Argamassa**, home to some large resort hotels. Just after the Nikki Beach Ibiza there are surviving sections (around 400m) of a **Roman stone aqueduct**, whose channelled water once fed a fish farm.

Just east of s'Argamassa is the sandy bay of **Cala Martina**.

⑥ Punta Arabí

From s'Argamassa you could explore the thickly wooded promontory of **Punta Arabí**, which sits opposite two tiny rocky islets – but there's no beach here. Or if you head along the road to Es Canar (a 15-minute stroll away) you'll pass Club Punta Arabí, where a huge, very touristy hippy market takes place each Wednesday.

Best Walks
Platja d'en Bossa to Platja de ses Salines

🏃 The Walk

This southern Ibizan walk cuts through a diverse landscape that takes in three of the island's best beaches and wooded hills, and fringes some salt flats. There are a couple of landmark defence towers to admire along the way, and the sea views are simply outstanding as you're never more than a few steps from the coast. People-watching is superb as both Salines and Cavallet attract more than their fair share of famous faces and flamboyant characters. In the summer, early morning or late afternoon are the best times to do this walk as there's very little shade once you're south of the pine woods.

Start South end of Platja d'en Bossa

Finish Northern end of Platja de ses Salines

Length 7km; three hours

🍴 Take a Break

Es Cavallet and Platja de ses Salines both have three beachside *chiringuitos*. On Salines, **Sa Trinxa** (p110) is our favourite. Over on Es Cavallet, **La Escollera** (p110) is great for seafood, while barefoot chic **El Chiringuito** (p92) and **Chiringay** (chiringay.com; snacks €7-10, meals €16-30; ⏰10am-10pm May-Oct) both offer healthy menus.

❶ Platja d'en Bossa

The southernmost part of **Platja d'en Bossa** (p107) is by far the most attractive stretch of this popular tourist beach, with large sand dunes and limited tourist development. On the eastern side of Bossa are some salt pans, and there are fine views back along the coast to Ibiza Town.

❷ Torre de Sal Rossa

At the extreme southern point of Plajta d'en Bossa, this conical defence tower was constructed in the 16th century to safeguard the island's salt trade. The bay just below, **Cala de sa Sal Rossa** (Pink Salt Cove), was a tiny port until the 19th century. Rowing boats loaded with salt would shuttle back and forth to cargo ships anchored offshore.

❸ Pine Woods

This next section of the walk offers some shade and leaves the tourism of Ibiza behind. From the tower a path climbs up the pine-forested hills. This well-defined, undulating track parallels the coast south for 3km, passing deserted rocky coves. The path doesn't stray more than 50m or so from the coast, so it's impossible to get lost.

❹ Es Cavallet

You eventually emerge at **Es Cavallet** (p107) beach, close to La Escollera restaurant. There's little shade ahead, so consider taking a break here. Next up it's a straight walk south along the shore. The southern end of the beach is very popular with gay visitors, and has a good restaurant: Chiringay.

❺ Punta de ses Portes

Beyond Chiringay the shoreline is rocky as you approach the **Punta de ses Portes**, the island's southernmost point. There's a tiny cove here ringed by fisher's huts, and amazing views over the sea south to Formentera. Guarding this point is the **Torre de ses Portes** (p103), another landmark defence tower.

❻ Platja de ses Salines

From the tower, you can return up the western side of this narrow peninsula towards **Platja de ses Salines** (p103). You'll pass several tiny coves and rocky outcrops. Salines beach is Ibiza's premier place to pose, so you'll encounter several places popular with the beautiful crowd. There's a bus stop at the north end of the beach.

Best
Beaches

Ibiza and Formentera are endowed with an astonishing number of beaches. There are white-sand wonders where you can kick back in serious style in a luxury beach club, and glorious undeveloped stretches of sand inside natural parks. You'll also find a staggering number of little coves – sandy, pebbly and rocky – dotted around the islands' coasts.

Best White-Sand Heaven

Trucador Peninsula The peninsula's exceptional back-to-back stretches of sand regularly rank in those 'World's Best Beaches' lists. Forming the eastern and western shores of Formentera's Trucador Peninsula, the white sands of Illetes and Llevant are lapped by Caribbean-esqe turquoise water. (p116)

Platja de ses Salines Backed by sand dunes and thickets of sabina pine trees, this undeveloped beach has a raw, natural beauty. Its *chiringuitos* (beach bars) are a prime hang-out for the rich and famous, fashionistas and wannabes. (p103)

Es Cavallet This wonderful beach is the most gay-friendly on the island, especially around the southern section, where you'll find the Chiringay bar/cafe/hang-out. Its northern shores have two excellent restaurants. (p107)

Platja de Migjorn Forming almost the entire southern shore of Formentera, this naked haven rarely gets too packed and is sporadically dotted with excellent barefoot-style *chiringuitos*. (p119)

Cala Conta No question, this fine beach has the clearest water in Ibiza and is a deservedly popular place to catch the sunset. (p85)

☑ **Top Tips**

▶ *Secret Beaches Ibiza* by Rob Smith is the definitive guide to the Ibizan coastline.

▶ Between November and April there are almost no beach bus services; a hire car (or bike) is essential for exploration.

▶ Sun lounges and umbrellas cost €5 to €8 (each) on most beaches. Beach clubs charge much more.

Aigües Blanques A slender stretch of sand beneath northeast Ibiza's coastal cliffs, this wild, naturist beach is washed by ocean-fresh waves (its name means 'white waters'). (p65)

Platja d'en Bossa Yes, the north end of this 3km-long stretch of sand is lined with concrete hotels, but the southern section is fringed with sand dunes and has several stylish bar-restaurants. (p107)

Best Delectable Coves

Cala d'en Serra Well off the beaten track in the far northeast of the island, this gem of a cove is ringed by hills and wooded headlands. (p65)

Benirràs Its situation, surrounded by high hills, is superb and there's a distinctly bohemian vibe. Visit on Sunday for a drumming ceremony to mark sunset. (p65)

Cala d'Hort A breathtaking sand-and-pebble cove with fine snorkelling and three good seafood restaurants. There are magnificent views of Es Vedrà, a soaring island directly offshore. (p99)

Cala Vedella A family-friendly beach that boasts a really sheltered shoreline of white sand. There are several attractive cafe-restaurants at the back of the bay. Also has bus connections to Ibiza Town and Sant Antoni. (p107)

Cala Saona A delightful cove beach on Formentera's western shore, Saona offers wonderful sunset views and is highly popular with families. (p119)

Best Remote & Rewarding

Cala Llentrisca Getting there is half the fun when it comes to this hidden bay, which is a short hike from the nearest road, below the lofty peak of Cap Llentrisca. (p107)

Portitxol On Ibiza's most remote coastline, this simply startling, totally undeveloped horseshoe-shaped cove lies below high hills and craggy cliffs. (p69)

s'Estanyol This is the nearest undeveloped *cala* to Ibiza Town. There are fine sands and you'll find a great *chiringuito* for meals and drinks. (p33)

Espalmador Just north of Formentera, the island of Espalmador has a sweeping, south-facing sandy cove, Platja de S'Alga, with turquoise-tinged water. It's only accessible by boat, or via a wade-swim from the north of the Trucador Peninsula. (p117)

Best
Eating

Best for Seafood

Es Torrent Expensive, but superb lobster and rice dishes. (p110)

Can Pujol Super-fresh seafood and sunset views. (p92)

Es Boldado With *that* view over *the* rock. (p109)

Restaurante Sa Caleta Fine fish dishes, and try their Caleta coffee. (p109)

Best Meat Feasts

El Parador Simple surrounds, expertly grilled meats. (p40)

Can Caus Locally sourced meats and moderate prices. (p75)

Es Rebost de Can Prats A great place to try Ibizan dishes. (p91)

Es Caliu Barbecued meats *par excellence*. (p75)

Cas Pagès For that really local experience. (p77)

Best Chiringuitos

El Bigotes Ibiza-style fish and seafood on a lonely cove beach. (p57)

Chiringuito Cala Xuclar A unique island experience in a simple fish shack. (p75)

El Chiringuito At the rear of a tiny cove; try their paella. (p92)

Best High-End Dining

La Paloma Everything an Ibizan restaurant should be. The food is cooked with love and consummate skill. (p77)

Amante Super-stylish place offering a refined atmosphere and lovely sea views. (p58)

Beach House Highly accomplished cooking and a lovely beachfront terrace. (p111)

Ama Lur Where Ibiza's old money comes to dine on Basque food. (p79)

Ca 'nAlfredo An Ibiza Town institution; the menu has an authentic island flavour. (p40)

Macao Cafe Excellent Italian cuisine; eat on the romantic garden terrace. (p67)

Sa Capella A stunning setting inside a converted chapel. (p92)

Best
Clubs

Believe the hype. Despite its status as a tiny island in the western Mediterranean, Ibiza can lay a strong claim to being the world's king of clubs. All the globe's top DJs play here in the summer months, and the clubbing industry is very much the engine room of the economy.

Pacha When Ibizans are asked about Pacha, their response is to reply with a glint in their eye, a smile and the phrase 'Pacha es Pacha'. Quite simply nowhere else on the island can match its class and cachet: it's beautifully designed with elegant terraces and alcoves, and myriad rooms and dance floors. (p43)

Space Totally renovated in the last decade, Space has two terraces, a vast main room and lots of quirky little corners like El Salón, which has an intimate vibe and eclectic music policy. In terms of dance music history, Space's place is confirmed; its terrace hosted the key parties of the 1990s. (p111)

Amnesia Steeped in Ibizan clubbing history, Amnesia was where DJ Alfredo first pioneered the Balearic Beat. Today there are two main rooms: the terrace is geared more to vocal house, while the main room has a darker, deeper ambience. (p47)

DC 10 *Very* close to the airport (incoming jets elicit whoops of delight on the dance floor), DC 10 is where you go to escape the celeb crowd and VIP areas that have proliferated in many other clubs. Retains an underground vibe and draws a music-savvy clubbing crowd. (p111)

PIXICA · GETTY IMAGES ©

☑ Top Tips

▶ Drink prices are outrageous, typically €8 to €12 for a beer or water, and €15 for a spirit and mixer.

▶ Discounted entrance tickets can be bought from bars all over the island.

▶ Use the **Discobus** (www.ibizabus.com/ ibiza/discobus) to cut transport costs.

Best
History

Ibiza is far more than superclubs and sandy beaches. The historic walled city of Dalt Vila is a Unesco World Heritage site and contains several museums of note. Each village has a landmark church, while the island's emblematic defence towers are a potent reminder of the once-omnipresent pirate menace.

Best Museums

Madina Yabisa La Cúria Up in Dalt Vila, this compact museum is dedicated to Ibiza's Moorish period. (p25)

Museu d'Art Contemporani Contemporary art with an island connection in a landmark building inside the old city. (p25)

Es Pujol An excellent private museum dedicated to Ibizan culture in remote Santa Agnès. (p72)

Necròpolis del Puig des Molins A fascinating Punic burial site and impressive museum close to Ibiza Town's centre. (p38)

Casa Broner The modernist home of an acclaimed architect, with lovely views from its terraces. (p29)

Museu Etnogràfic This old farmhouse in Santa Eulària superbly showcases Ibiza's rural heritage. (p53)

Best Churches

Catedral Built in Catalan Gothic style, high above the capital. (p26)

Església de Puig de Missa Looks over Santa Eulària, and includes its own defence tower. (p53)

Església de Sant Jordí In an unlikely suburban location, this historic church boasts full battlements. (p108)

Església de Sant Miquel A historic church in the north where traditional dances are performed. (p71)

Església de Sant Xavier A brooding fortress-style structure in Formentera's Sant Francesc. (p120)

Església de Sant Carles A whitewashed 18th-century building which once witnessed holy murder. (p63)

Best Defence Towers

Torre des Savinar Hike up to this tower which offers unparalleled views over Es Vedrà and the southern coastline. (p99)

Torre d'en Valls Enjoys a stunning, remote location in Ibiza's northeast, with views over Tagomago. (p63)

Torre de ses Portes Defines the deep south of Ibiza, with vistas south to Formentera and Espalmador. (p103)

Best
Secret Spots

Ibiza attracts two million tourists a year, but you'll always be able to find a remote spot if you've the inclination to get off the main roads and prime your sense of discovery.

EVAIILA / GETTY IMAGES ©

Best Coves

Cala Saldeta The little sister of Cala Salada can only be reached by scrambling over some fisher's huts. (p85)

Cala des Moltons Not visible from Port de Sant Miquel, but just metres around the coast. (p69)

Port de ses Caletes At the end of a rough road you'll find this hidden northern bay. (p69)

Cala d'Aubarca Hoof it on foot to reach this broad, exposed bay in Ibiza's northwest. (p69)

Es Torrent An idyllic little cove at the foot of a river valley on the south coast. (p107)

Best Offbeat Spots

Ses Feixes Fields that the Moors developed for crops and fruit, on the fringe of Ibiza Town. (p33)

Casita Verde This remote eco-centre promotes sustainable farming and welcomes visitors (Sundays only). (p48)

Portinatx Lighthouse So far north it's almost in Mallorca, and reached by a lovely coastal hike. (p74)

Stonehenge Utterly extraordinary contemporary sculpture on a remote rocky coastline in Ibiza's southwest. (p105)

Sant Francesc de s'Estany Blink and you'll miss this tiny settlement by the salt pans. (p104)

Best Caves

Cova des Cuieram Intriguing cave-temple dedicated to the goddess Tanit, in the far north of Ibiza. (p73)

Cova des Mirador Just below the main Vedrà lookout, this cave has inspirational views. (p100)

Cova de Buda Perched above Atlantis, this cave contains a beautiful image of the Buddha. (p100)

Best
Villages

For an authentic flavour of island life away from the tourist resorts and popular beaches, drop by one of Ibiza or Formentera's villages. Each boasts a landmark church and a local bar or two, and is the focus of a wider rural community.

Santa Gertrudis de Fruitera Once famous for its surrounding orchards, today this village is better known for its amazing selection of cafes, bars and restaurants – from local drinking haunts to destination dining. While you're here check out the auction house and village church. (p66)

Sant Francesc Xavier Tiny Sant Francesc has really up-and-come in the last decade and now has an array of boutiques that cater perfectly to Formentera's brand of barefoot living. Explore the area around the village square with its fortress-church and myriad cafe-bars. (p124)

Sant Carles de Peralta Yes, it's tiny, but this village is home to a famous bar (Anita's; p80), a striking village church, and a little shopping

zone just east of the centre where you'll find a quirky boutique or two to browse. (p62)

Sant Joan de Labritja If you're exploring the north of Ibiza, Sant Joan is a mandatory stop. There's a cute little main street of cottage-like houses and two good bar-restaurants here (one very local, the other totally cosmopolitan). (p80)

Sant Josep de sa Talaia Capital of the south of the island, Sant Josep is worth a wander, with its imposing village church, a good tapas place, and the live music venue Racó Verd. (p105)

Sant Rafel Better known for the clubs on its doorstep, Sant Rafel also has a tranquil side and some tempting restaurants and cafes. There are stunning views to the east from its village church. (p46)

Best
For Families

Dalt Vila All kids love castles, and this walled city feels like a huge one, with its stupendous defensive walls, ramparts, bastions and towers. Enter via the Portal de ses Taules for maximum effect – you'll pass over a drawbridge and through a triple gateway. Check out the Madina Yabisa La Cúria museum while you're here. (p24)

Aguamar (Platja d'en Bossa; ◷10am-5.30pm May-Sep; adult/child €18.50/10) This fun water park is very family-oriented and has impressive chutes and slides that are sure to put a smile on everyone's face. Standout attractions are the Kamikaze and Black Hole. There are paddling areas for very small children, and ample snack bars and drink stands.

Boat Trips An excursion by boat to Formentera is a wonderful day out for all, with the thrill of the sea journey quickening the pulse. Or, if you don't want a full day trip, catch a ride on one of the little 'water taxis' which connect all the main towns, resorts and beaches in Ibiza. (p148)

Aquarium Cap Blanc Just north of Sant Antoni this small open-air aquarium has a series of fish tanks containing plenty of local fish, crabs, lobsters, eels and even a small shark. (p89)

Cala Bassa If you're on the west side of the island this beautiful cove beach is well worth a visit. You'll find lots of activities (including pedalos for hire and banana boat rides). (p85)

LATITUDESTOCK – STUART PEARCE / GETTY IMAGES ©

☑ **Top Tips**

▶ Many restaurants in Spain don't open until 8pm in the evening, so if you've hungry young mouths to feed plan accordingly.

▶ Consider buying your own beach parasol on the first day of a holiday as they typically cost €5 to €8 to hire per day.

Best
Bars

Bar action is spread around the islands. Ibiza Town's Port Area has dozens of cool spots, and also a gay village. Sant Antoni has a world-famous Sunset Strip of bars. And dotted around Ibiza and Formentera are *chiringuitos* (beach bars) and atmospheric village inns.

SCOTT E BARBOUR / GETTY IMAGES ©

Best Hip Bars

Bar 1805 A cocktail mecca in gritty Sa Penya with lots of absinthe action. (p35)

KM5 A supremely elegant garden lounge in a rural location; draws a beautiful crowd. (p111)

Ibiza Rocks House at Pike's Hotel Recreate the Club Tropicana vibe in situ at this legendary venue close to Sant Antoni. (p92)

The Rock Mix with the clubbing in-crowd on the harbourfront terrace at this buzzing Port Area favourite. (p35)

Sunrise Zany bar in the capital's gay village which attracts a hip crowd – check out the swings. (p35)

Best Local Bars

Anita's A great village inn: try its homemade *hierbas* liquor and enjoy the social vibe. (p80)

Fonda Pepe Get all nostalgic for the 1960s in this legendary hippy hang-out. (p123)

Madagascar Boasts one of Ibiza Town's best terraces and has very reasonable drink prices. (p39)

Best Beach Bars

Sa Trinxa Salines' best *chiringuito* has a totally mellow ambience, and DJs play Balearic sounds. (p130)

Beach House Gaze over the waves from a Bali beach bed while DJs spin their stuff. (p111)

Café del Mar San An's original sunset bar boasts a prime location and is still going strong. (p87)

Best
Outdoor Activities

With a benign climate and sparkling, unpolluted seas, Ibiza and Formentera are perfect for lovers of the great outdoors.

ULTRAMARINFOTO / GETTY IMAGES ©

Walking Ibiza (📞608 692901; www.walkingibiza.com) Hit the trails of Ibiza's coast and interior with pro guide Toby. His guided walks cover everything from community hikes in winter (suggested donation €10) to three-day treks (€300) and two-week around-the-island treks (€1400).

Orcasub (📞971 80 63 07; www.orcasub.es; Hotel Tarida Beach, Cala Tarida; snorkelling €35, fun dives from €50) These PADI professionals dive off Ibiza's southwestern coast at sites including Es Vedrà. All kinds of courses are available, from Open Water to advanced tech training. Snorkelling and boat excursions are also offered.

Ibiza MTB (📞616 129929; www.ibizamtb.com) Ibiza has some fantastic mountain-bike terrain. Slip into the saddle for three-hour guided mountain-bike tours, which reach from the west coast to forest single tracks and sunset rides. Rents bikes, too (€15 to €50).

Ibiza Horse Valley (📞680 624911; www.ibizahorsevalley.com; Sant Joan de Labritja) Nestled in a lush valley near Sant Joan, this sanctuary and riding centre for mistreated horses offers everything from half-day treks into the hills to camping with horses and beach hacks.

Wet4Fun (📞971 32 18 09; www.wet4fun.com; Carrer Roca Plana 51; 🕙10am-6pm Mon-Sat, 2-6pm Sun May-Oct) Formentera-based Wet4Fun offers the chance to learn windsurfing, paddle-surfing, catamaran sailing, canoeing and kayaking. You can also rent out canoes (€10 per hour) and bicycles (€25 for four days) here.

Ibiza Mundo Activo (📞676 075704; www.ibizamundoactivo.blogspot.co.uk) This one-stop adventure-sports shop takes you hiking, biking, caving, climbing, stand-up paddle boarding and kayaking across the island.

Best
Rural Hotels

There are around 30 rural hotels (*agroturisme*) in Ibiza and a couple in Formentera – most are converted farmhouses. Because the islands are very small, none are particularly remote. For tranquillity and escapism they can't be beat, though this does come at a considerable cost.

Can Xuxu (www.canxuxu.com; Crta Sant Josep–Cala Tarida Km 4; r from €140; 🍴❄️@🛜🏊) The owner Alex and his staff really make this place, doting on guests and preparing homemade food and drinks. There's a lovely, very private pool area. Book one of the converted Javan teak houses for an utterly memorable stay.

Can Pere (📞971 19 66 00; www.canpereibiza.com; r from €165; ❄️@🛜🏊) Boasts an astonishing hilltop location surrounded by pine woods, with magnificent vistas from its pool – you can really relax here. Rooms and suites are tastefully presented and there's a fine in-house restaurant.

Can Lluc (📞971 19 86 73; www.canlluc.com; Ctra Sant Rafel–Santa Agnès Km 2; d incl breakfast from €371; 🍴❄️@🛜🏊) In Ibiza's isolated northwest, this beautifully appointed rural hotel offers total tranquillity. There are wonderful grounds, with Bali beds around the pool. Service is attentive and there's a good restaurant.

Can Pujolet (📞971 80 51 70; www.canpujolet.com; Santa Inés; r €160-290, apt €380-490; ❄️🛜🏊) Swap partying for pin-drop peace at dreamy Can Pujolet, 4km northwest of Sant Mateu. Rooms play up simple luxury with exposed stone and terraces rising from the olive groves. The property's organic fruit and veg end up on the dinner table.

Atzaró (📞971 33 88 38; www.atzaro.com; Crta Sant Joan Km 15; d €390-440, ste €510-810; ❄️🛜🏊) Combining Japanese Zen with tribal Africa and farmhouse Ibiza, Atzaró is the ultimate in rural luxury. Its stunning rooms feature new-wave design flourishes; some rooms have private terraces and four-poster beds. There's a well-regarded restaurant and an astoundingly lovely spa. Prices shown are high-season rates; rooms cost as little as €120 in winter.

Can Talaias (📞971 33 57 42; www.hotelcantalaias.com; Ctra Sant Carles–Cala Boix; d from €188; ⏰ Apr-Oct; ❄️@🛜🏊) The former home of English actor Terry-Thomas, this *agroturisme* is located atop a hill surrounded by pine forests and with views over the sea. A stay here is all about peace and relaxing in the gardens.

Can Curreu (971 33 52 80; www.cancurreu. com; Ctra de Sant Carles Km 12; d incl breakfast from €275; ✿ @ 🛜 🌊) Above terraces of almond trees, this much modified Ibizan farmstead has exquisitely decorated and furnished rooms. Room rates include access to the relaxing spa with its multiple facilities.

Can Planells (971 33 49 24; www.canplanells. com; Carrer de Venda Rubió 2; d incl breakfast €175-220, ste €220-300; ✿ 🛜 🌊)

This country mansion near Sant Miquel exudes relaxed rural luxury in its handful of tastefully arranged doubles and suites (the best have private terraces). Farm-fresh produce makes breakfast a bit special.

Es Pas (687 807819; www.espasformentera.com; Cami des Arenals; r from €170; ✿ @ 🛜 🌊) Close to Formentera's Es Caló bay, this rural hotel enjoys a peaceful location, and has a fine pool and gardens, perfect for zoning out with a book. You can stroll to both north- and south-coast beaches from here.

Ca Sa Vilda Marge (971 33 32 34; www. casavildamarge.com; Ctra de Portinatx; incl breakfast

s €98-139, d €149-169, f €259; ✿ @ 🛜 🌊) This petite rural guesthouse is a little slice of heaven, with owners who really aim to please. The quiet rooms are done out in natural hues, floaty drapes, beams and exposed stone. It's located 2km off the main C733 towards Portinatx.

IMAGEBROKER / ALAMY ©

Can Planells

Best
Sunsets

The sunset is a big deal in Ibiza and Formentera. DJ José Padilla, resident at the Café del Mar for years, is arguably the person most responsible for this with his phenomenal downbeat music selections. Search for the original vibe on Sant Antoni's Sunset Strip, or head off-piste and create your own...

LUNAMARINA / GETTY IMAGES ©

Best in Ibiza

Torre des Savinar The perfect viewing spot to take in the majesty of Es Vedrà. (p99)

Stonehenge Savour a virgin coastline and Andrew Rogers' inspirational sculpture. (p105)

Sunset Strip The classic sunset spot in Sant Antoni; choose from a selection of bars. (p94)

Benirràs Top choice in the north, especially on Sundays when the drummers congregate. (p65)

Cala Conta Islands dot the horizon from this lovely beach in western Ibiza. (p85)

Kumharas Enjoy the world music and boho vibe at this popular bar in Sant Antoni bay. (p93)

Salines Salt Pans At sunset these pools are painted a kaleidoscopic palette of pinkish reds. (p103)

Cala Salada A great choice in the winter months; the sun sets between islands offshore. (p85)

Best in Formentera

Cap de Barbària The lunar landscape around this remote lighthouse adds drama to the occasion. (p119)

Restaurante El Mirador Watch the sun sink over the hourglass-like outline of Formentera from this elevated position. (p122)

Cala Saona The cliffs around this bay are the perfect vantage point for sunset. (p119)

☑ **Top Tips**

▶ A bespoke, memorable experience, www.ibizasecret picnic.com offers sunset chilling in remote settings. DJ Jonny Lee sets up decks and sofas by the coast, mixes drinks, serves grub and organises transport.

Survival Guide

Survival Guide

Before You Go

When to Go

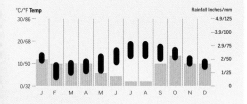

→ Spring (Feb–May)
Spectacular almond
blossoms in February.
Resorts open for busi-
ness in early May.

→ Summer (Jun–Sep)
Tourist season is in full
swing. By August the
islands are packed and
humidity is very high.

→ Autumn (Oct–Nov)
The season winds down
by early October. Sea
temperatures remain
mild.

→ Winter (Dec–Jan)
Locals rest up and
concentrate on family
matters around Christ-
mas. Mild, even warmish
days of 20°C are not
uncommon.

Book Your Stay

☑ It's essential to reserve
well ahead in August.

Useful Websites

→ Ibiza Hotel Guide (www.
ibizahotelsguide.com) Official
website of Ibiza's hoteliers
association.

→ Ibiza Lodge (www.ibiza-
lodge.es) Apartments to
rent at moderate rates in
both Ibiza and Formentera.

→ Ibiza Spotlight (www.
ibizaspotlight.com) Hotels,
apartments and villas in
Ibiza.

→ Lonely Planet (www.
lonelyplanet.com) Author
recommendation reviews
and online booking.

→ White Ibiza (www.white-
ibiza.com) Upmarket hotels
and accommodation.

Best Budget

→ La Dama de Ibiza (www.
ladamadeibiza.com) Simple
yet stylish place right in
the heart of the capital's

rt Area action. Bathoms are shared.

Hostal Boix (www.
stalcalaboix.es) Right
lovely Cala de Boix
Ibiza's northeast, this
ostal couldn't be further
om the Ibiza madness.
ruced up in 2013,
any rooms have sea
ews.

Hostal Sa Rota (www.
stalsarota.com) Bargain
ostal in Santa Eulària
at has bright, generous
oms with modern bath
shower.

Es Alocs (www.hostal
cs.com) Friendly choice
at sits on the beach
Figueral. Rooms oc-
py two floors and most
ve a small fridge and
lcony.

Vara de Rey (www.hibiza.
m) In a restored Ibiza
wn mansion, this boho-
voured guesthouse is
cated on tree-lined Vara
Rey.

st Midrange

Apartamentos Roselló
ww.apartamentosrosello.
m) Situated just south
Dalt Vila, these apart-
ents enjoy stupendous
ean-facing views. Try
reserve in the newly
novated block.

⟶ **Hostal Parque** (www.
hostalparque.com) Over-
looks Ibiza Town's palm-
dotted Plaça des Parc
and has inviting, modern
rooms.

⟶ **Hotel Calador** (www.
calador-ibiza.com) Offering
amazing Vedrà vistas, this
large complex has sunny
rooms and apartments
(most with sea-facing
terraces), palm-fringed
gardens, a pool and ten-
nis courts.

⟶ **Hostal Illes Pitiüses**
(www.illespitiuses.com) It's
on the busy main drag
in Formentera's Sant
Ferran, but this clean,
friendly place is decent
value. Prices almost halve
in the low season.

Best Top End

⟶ **Hotel La Ventana**
(www.laventanaibiza.com)
A historic 15th-century
mansion inside Dalt Vila,
where many rooms come
with four-poster beds and
there's a lovely roof terrace and restaurant.

⟶ **Urban Spaces Ibiza**
(urbanspacesibiza.com) Ibiza
Town hipster hang-out
with roomy, mural-
splashed suites, proper
workstations, and balco-
nies with terrific views.

Rural Hotels
Ibiza and Formen-
tera have some
excellent rural
hotels (p142).

⟶ **Es Marès** (www.hotel
esmares.com) A slinky boutique hotel that exudes
Formenteran barefoot
beach chic. Its all-white
rooms are dressed with
funky driftwood and lo-
cally quarried sandstone.

⟶ **Can Gall** (www.agro
cangall.com) A 200-year-old
finca (ranch) near Balàfia
set amid citrus and olive
groves. The rooms play up
rural luxury, with wooden
ceilings and exposed
stone.

Arriving in Ibiza

☑ For the best way to get
to your accommodation,
see p17.

Ibiza Airport
Ibiza's airport is in the
south of the island. It's
extremely busy during
the main tourist season
and very quiet in winter.

Taxi

➔ There's a taxi rank right outside arrivals. Between mid-July and the end of August there are long queues and you may have to wait up to an hour for a ride. Typical fares from the airport:

Ibiza Town €16

Sant Antoni €27

Sant Joan €34

➔ Check www.ibizaairport. org for sample fares. Fares increase after 9pm.

➔ Always use official taxis; 'pirate' drivers hang around at the airport but use unlicensed cars.

Bus

L10 Connects the airport with Ibiza Town (every 15 to 30 minutes, 6.20am to midnight).

L9 Links the airport with Sant Josep and Sant Antoni (June to mid-October, hourly 8am to 1am, until 3am in July and August).

L24 Connects the airport with Santa Eulària and Es Canar (June to September, hourly 7am to 11pm).
 You can check schedules at www.ibizabus.com.

Hire Car

Companies including Hertz and Avis have offices at the airport. There are many other car-rental agencies in the vicinity but you'll have to use their complimentary shuttle bus services, which is time consuming.

La Savina, Formentera

There's no airport in Formentera. The only point of entry is the ferry port of La Savina, which has excellent facilities including a tourist office inside its modern passenger terminal.

Taxi From the port typical fares are: Sant Francesc €8; Platja de Migjorn €16; and La Mola €25.

Bus Buses run from the port to the island's main villages (p150).

Bicycle and Motorbike You'll find many rental places by the ferry terminal; prices hardly vary (p150).

Getting Around

Bicycle

☑ **Best for** getting around Formentera, and exploring country lanes in Ibiza.

➔ Flat Formentera is perfectly set up for cyclists

➔ The Ibiza tourist board has prepared 21 cycling routes around the island ranging from easy rides to tough climbs. Consult www.ibiza.travel/en/cicloturismo.php for downloadable PDFs and GPX formats.

➔ **Ibiza MTB** (☎616 129929; www.ibizamtb.com) rents quality bikes and offers guided rides.

Boat

☑ **Best for** getting to Formentera, and for seeing the coast of Ibiza.

➔ Passenger ferries run between Ibiza Town and La Savina every 30 to 45 minutes; journey time is 30 to 60 minutes.

➔ There are discounts for children.

Car transportation costs are expensive; it's better to hire a vehicle on arrival in Formentera.

There are far fewer sailings between November and April.

The following ferries sail between Ibiza Town's harbour and La Savina, Formentera:

Aqua Bus (www.aquabus ferryboats.com) Operates budget-priced ferry service (nine daily May to October) for €19 return.

Baleària (www.balearia. com) Up to 18 daily. Foot passengers pay from €17.50 one way. Bicycles are free.

Mediterranea Pitiusa (www.mediterraneapitiusa. com) Up to 15 daily; passengers only; fast and slow boats; €30 to €40.

Trasmapi (www.trasmapi. com) Operates ferries every 30 minutes (8.30am to midnight) in summer. Passengers pay €43 return.

Aqua Bus also runs boats to Formentera (many via Espalmador) from many different Ibiza resorts. These are slow-ish boats (most over an hour) but economical (€18 to €26 return).

Bus
☑ **Best for** saving costs.

➡ Plan your trip carefully at www.ibizabus.com as services are infrequent, except on the main routes.

➡ Fares to most destinations are between €2 and €3.50; there's a small surplus to/from the airport.

➡ The excellent **Discobus** (www.discobusibiza.com) allows all-night travel at a reasonable cost. It's very popular with clubbers and connects Ibiza Town, Sant Antoni, Platja d'en Bossa, Sant Rafel and Santa Eulària.

Hire Car
☑ **Best for** exploring Ibiza, and convenience.

➡ You'll only be able to get to the islands' most remote places if you have your own wheels.

➡ Many places (including some rural hotels) are only accessible via dirt roads. Drive carefully and be aware that rental companies' insurance often won't

Boat Trips Around Ibiza
Buzzing around the Ibizan coast on a boat with the wind in your hair can't be beat. Many resorts and towns offer these 'water taxi' connections (May to October only); there are usually seven to 10 boats daily. Routes include Sant Antoni to Cala Bassa, Cala Conta, Es Canar and Santa Eulària via several east coast beaches. Check routes and schedules at www. aquabusferryboats. com.

cover you for damage to undercarriages.

➡ Parking spots are in very short supply in Ibiza Town in summer; consider using alternative transport instead.

➡ Local rental companies include **Ok Rent-a-Car** (www.okrentacar.es), **Gold Car** (www.goldcar.es) and **Moto Luis** (www.motoluis. com).

Getting Around Formentera

➡ Bicycles (€6 to €10 per day), motorbikes (€20 to €30) and cars (from €35) are available from rental outlets in La Savina and Es Pujols. 'Green route' cycling maps are available from tourist offices.

➡ Taxis are quite costly in Formentera (p17). Taxi numbers:

Es Pujols ☎971 32 80 16

La Savina ☎971 32 20 02

Sant Francesc ☎971 32 20 16

➡ Bus schedules vary considerably according to the time of year, with a minimum of eight daily between May and October, more in July to August. Regular bus tickets cost €1.80 to €2.55. For bus schedules consult www.busformentera.com.

Bus L1 La Sabina–Sant Francesc–Sant Ferran–Es Pujols

Bus L2 La Sabina–Sant Francesc–Sant Ferran–La Mola

Bus L3 These 'tourist circuit' buses cost more than regular buses (€6 to €12), but do make stops for photographs.

Taxi

☑ **Best for** those that like a tipple.

➡ Taxi numbers:

Ibiza Town ☎971 39 83 40

Sant Antoni ☎971 34 37 64

Sant Joan ☎971 33 33 33

Sant Josep ☎971 80 00 80

Santa Eulària ☎971 33 30 33

➡ Taxis can be in very short supply in July and August.

➡ There's a minimum fare of €4.95 if you book by phone, plus €1.09 per km. Rates rise after 9pm.

➡ There's no extra charge for luggage.

➡ A green light indicates the taxi is for hire.

On Foot

☑ **Best for** Ibiza Town.

➡ The Port Area of Ibiza Town and Dalt Vila are best explored on foot, though the latter occupies a steep hill. There are fine promenades in Santa Eulària and Sant Antoni.

➡ Hikers should check out **Walking Ibiza** (www.walkingibiza.com) for guided walks.

➡ For two good island walks, see p128.

Essential Information

Business Hours

Banks 8am to 2pm Monday to Friday

Post Offices 8.30am to 8pm Monday to Friday

Restaurants Hours vary considerably. In beach resorts casual places open 8am to 11pm May to October. Elsewhere across islands it's 1pm to 4pm and 8pm to 11.30pm.

...ops 10am to 9pm,
...en until midnight June
...September

...ectricity

220V/230V/50Hz

...nergencies

...neral emergencies
112

...bulance ☏061

...e service ☏080

...lice ☏091

...cal Police ☏092

...oney
Virtually every village
both islands has at
...st one ATM.

...rrency Euro (€)

...edit and Debit Cards
...n be used in most

shops, restaurants,
hotels, clubs and super-
markets in both Ibiza and
Formentera. However,
don't expect to pay for a
sun lounge on the beach
with plastic, and some
small bars only take cash.

Public Holidays

New Year's Day 1 January

Epiphany 6 January

Balearics Day 1 March

Good Friday Late March/
April

Easter Monday Late
March/April

Labour Day 1 May

St James (Formentera)
26 July

St Mary 5 August

St Ciriac 8 August

Assumption Day
15 August

Hispanic Day 12 October

All Saints Day
1 November

Constitution Day
6 December

**Immaculate Conception
Day** 8 December

Christmas Day
25 December

Money-Saving Tips

➡ Use buses or hire
a bicycle to get
around.

➡ *Tostadas* or
bocadillos (both
sandwiches) are
cheap (€2 to €5) in
cafes. Three-course
lunchtime set meals
are often €10 to €12.

➡ Buy discounted
club tickets in
advance online, or
from authorised
merchants and bars
in resorts.

➡ Don't travel in
peak season (late
June to early Sep-
tember). Hotel rates
plummet outside
these times.

Telephones

Mobile Phones
☑ Consider purchasing a
local SIM to cut costs.

➡ Most mobile phones
will function fine in Ibiza,
but always check with
your provider that your
phone is enabled for use
abroad.

➡ Data roaming costs have
dropped considerably for
those with EU phones,

but can be very expensive for those from outside Europe.

Phone Codes

➡ **International access code** ☏ 00

➡ **Spain country code** ☏ 34

Toilets

Toilets are few and far between. Popular beaches, including Talamanca and Salines, have public toilets, but more remote coves do not.

Generally, it's best to use toilet facilities in cafes or restaurants.

Tourist Information

☑ The official tourist information sites are www.ibiza.travel and www.formentera.es.

All the following offices have shorter hours in winter:

La Sabina, Formentera (☏ 971 32 20 57; www.formentera.es; Carrer de Calpe; ⊙ 9am-7pm Mon-Fri, to 3pm Sat & Sun May-Oct, 10am-2pm & 5-7pm Mon-Fri Nov-Apr) There are smaller branches in Es Pujols and opposite the church in Sant Francesc Xavier.

Ibiza Town Main Office (Map p36, D3; ☏ 971 30 19 00; www.ibiza.travel; Passeig de Vara de Rey 1; ⊙ 9am-8pm Mon-Sat, to 2pm Sun, shorter hours in winter)

Ibiza Town, Dalt Vila (Map p36, E5; ☏ 971 39 92 32; www.eivissa.es; Plaça de la Catedral; ⊙ 10am-2pm & 6-9pm Mon-Sat, 10am-2pm Sun)

Sant Antoni (☏ 971 34 3 63; visit.santantoni.net; Passeig de ses Fonts; ⊙ 9.30am-7.30pm Mon-Fri, to 2pm Sat & Sun, shorter hrs Nov-Apr) Beside the harbour.

Santa Eulària (☏ 971 33 07 28; www.santaeularia desriu.com; Carrer Mariano Riquer 4; ⊙ 9am-8pm Mon-Fri, to 2pm Sat)

Language

...th Spanish (more precisely known
..*castellano*, or Castilian) and Catalan
..*talà*, spoken in Catalonia) are official
..nguages in Spain. Eivissenc is the na-
.. dialect of Catalan spoken on Ibiza
..d Formentera. You'll be perfectly well
..derstood speaking Spanish in Ibiza
..d you'll find that most locals will
..ppily speak Spanish to you, especially
..ce they realise you're a foreigner.
..ere we've provided you with some
..anish to get you started, as well as
..me Catalan basics at the end.
..Just read our pronunciation guides
.. if they were English and you'll be
..derstood. Note that (m/f) indicates
..asculine and feminine forms.
..To enhance your trip with a phrase-
..ok, visit **lonelyplanet.com**. Lonely
..anet iPhone phrasebooks are avail-
..le through the Apple App store.

..asics

..ello.
.ola. | o·la

..odbye.
.iós. | a·dyos

..w are you?
.ué tal? | ke tal

..e, thanks.
..en, gracias. | byen gra·thyas

..ease.
.r favor. | por fa·vor

..ank you.
.acias. | gra·thyas

..cuse me.
..rdón. | per·don

..rry.
. siento. | lo syen·to

..s./No.
./No. | see/no

Do you speak (English)?
¿Habla (inglés)? | a·bla (een·gles)

I (don't) understand.
Yo (no) entiendo. | yo (no) en·tyen·do

Eating & Drinking

I'm a vegetarian. (m/f)
Soy | soy
vegetariano/a. | ve·khe·ta·rya·no/a

Cheers!
¡Salud! | sa·loo

That was delicious!
¡Estaba | es·ta·ba
buenísimo! | bwe·nee·see·mo

Please bring the bill.
Por favor nos | por fa·vor nos
trae la cuenta. | tra·e la kwen·ta

I'd like ...
Quisiera ... | kee·sye·ra ...

a coffee	un café	oon ka·fe
a table for two	una mesa para dos	oo·na me·sa pa·ra dos
a wine	un vino	oon vee·no
two beers	dos cervezas	dos ther·ve·thas

Shopping

I'd like to buy ...
Quisiera | kee·sye·ra
comprar ... | kom·prar ...

May I look at it?
¿Puedo verlo? | pwe·do ver·lo

How much is it?
¿Cuánto cuesta? | kwan·to kwes·ta

That's too/very expensive.
Es muy caro. | es mooy ka·ro

Can you lower the price?
¿Podría bajar | po·dree·a ba·khar
un poco | oon po·ko
el precio? | el pre·thyo

Emergencies

Help!
¡Socorro!   so·ko·ro

Call a doctor!
¡Llame a   lya·me a oon
un médico!   me·dee·ko

Call the police!
¡Llame a   lya·me a
la policía!   la po·lee·thee·a

I'm lost. (m/f)
Estoy perdido/a.   es·toy per·dee·do/a

I'm ill. (m/f)
Estoy enfermo/a.   es·toy en·fer·mo/a

Where are the toilets?
¿Dónde están   don·de es·tan
los baños?   los ba·nyos

Time & Numbers

What time is it?
¿Qué hora es?   ke o·ra es

It's (10) o'clock.
Son (las diez).   son (las dyeth)

morning	*mañana*	ma·nya·na
afternoon	*tarde*	tar·de
evening	*noche*	no·che
yesterday	*ayer*	a·yer
today	*hoy*	oy
tomorrow	*mañana*	ma·nya·na

1	*uno*	oo·no
2	*dos*	dos
3	*tres*	tres
4	*cuatro*	kwa·tro
5	*cinco*	theen·ko
6	*seis*	seys
7	*siete*	sye·te
8	*ocho*	o·cho
9	*nueve*	nwe·ve
10	*diez*	dyeth

Transport & Directions

Where's ...?
¿Dónde está ...?   don·de es·ta ...

What's the address?
¿Cuál es la   kwal es la
dirección?   dee·rek·thyon

Can you show me (on the map)?
¿Me lo puede   me lo pwe·de
indicar   een·dee·kar
(en el mapa)?   (en el ma·pa)

I want to go to ...
Quisiera ir a ...   kee·sye·ra eer a ...

What time does it arrive/leave?
¿A qué hora   a ke o·ra
llega/sale?   lye·ga/sa·le

I want to get off here.
Quiero bajarme   kye·ro ba·khar·me
aquí.   a·kee

Catalan – Basics

Good morning.
Bon dia.   bon dee·a

Good afternoon.
Bona tarda.   bo·na tar·da

Good evening.
Bon vespre.   bon bes·pra

Goodbye.
Adéu.   a·the·oo

Please.
Sisplau.   sees·pla·oo

Thank you.
Gràcies.   gra·see·a

You're welcome.
De res.   de res

Excuse me.
Perdoni.   par·tho·nee

I'm sorry.
Ho sento.   oo sen·to

How are you?
Com estàs?   kom as·tas

Very well.
(Molt) Bé.   (mol) be

ndex

See also separate subindexes for:

⊗ **Eating p157**

⊙ **Drinking p158**

✪ **Entertainment p158**

⊙ **Shopping p158**

Experiences 000
Map Pages 000

Behind the Scenes

Send Us Your Feedback

We love to hear from travellers – your comments help make our books better. We read every word, and we guarantee that your feedback goes straight to the authors. Visit **lonelyplanet.com/contact** to submit your updates and suggestions.

Note: We may edit, reproduce and incorporate your comments in Lonely Planet products such as guidebooks, websites and digital products, so let us know if you don't want your comments reproduced or your name acknowledged. For a copy of our privacy policy visit lonelyplanet.com/privacy.

Iain's Thanks

Sincere thanks to Martin Davies for his expert contacts and all-round island expertise, Andy and Chrissie Wilson for their friendship and good times, Jonny Lee, Paul and Julia, the Roselló family and Enrique Moreno. And to Fiona and my sons Louis and Monty for sharing the islands with me; may there be many more trips to come.

Acknowledgments

Cover photograph: Cala d'Hort beach, Ibiza, Michele Falzone/AWL

Photograph on pp4-5: Ibiza Town, Marco Simoni/Getty

This Book

This 1st edition of *Pocket Ibiza* was researched and written by Iain Stewart. This guidebook was produced by the following:

Destination Editor Lorna Parkes **Product Editors** Jenna Myers, Martine Power **Senior Cartographer** Anthony Phelan **Book Designer** Cam Ashley **Assisting Editors** Imogen Bannister, Anne Mulvaney **Cover Researcher** Campbell McKenzie **Thanks to** Sasha Baskett, Jo Cooke, Andi Jones, Karyn Noble, Angela Tinson, Tony Wheeler

Our Writer

Iain Stewart

Iain Stewart has been visiting Ibiza and Formentera since 1997 and considers the islands his spiritual home (and future abode). He's walked virtually the entire coastline of Ibiza, and spent many a happy hour researching the islands' history (and dance floors). He can think of no more perfect start to the day than a *café con leche* and a *tostada* in Ibiza Town followed by a hike to a remote cove beach. Iain lives in Brighton, UK and has written or co-written over 20 guidebooks for Lonely Planet.

Published by Lonely Planet Publications Pty Ltd
ABN 36 005 607 983
1st edition – Dec 2015
ISBN 978 1 74360 712 1
© Lonely Planet 2015 Photographs © as indicated 2015
10 9 8 7 6 5 4 3
Printed in China